# Praise for Eric Stanway

"Eric Stanway is kind of a local legend."
— *Virginia Prescott, "Word of Mouth,"*
*New Hampshire Public Radio*

### The Old Rindge House
"His intent, though, was not to create his own story line. It was, he said, to show that history 'isn't just names and dates in dusty old books, but the lives of real people.' He also wanted to, as a Dickens' character said, 'make your flesh creep.' He accomplishes both."
— *Barbara Coles, New Hampshire Magazine*

### Madame Sherri
"I grew up in this area. What a great read! Informative, interesting and fun! I am so glad I got this book!"
— *Amazon reviewer*

### Mysteries of Monadnock
"His latest collection of reports about ghosts, revenge, hauntings, spooky cemeteries and unsolved murders go straight to the New Englander penchant for white-eye reading."
— *Steve Sherman, The Keene Sentinel*

**Also by Eric Stanway**

History on a Plate
Another Course
The Old Rindge House
Vintage Blood Vol. 1
Vintage Blood Vol. 2
Madame Sherri
The Blood is the Life
Mad Ghosts and Englishmen
Mysteries of Monadnock
Cannibal of the Mountains
Stone-Cold Murder
The Victorian
Yuletide Spiritis
The Treasure of Dungeon Rock
Madame Sherri — The Special Edition *(with David Fiske)*
Haunted Hillsborough County
Cranks
Dark Tales of Gardner
Bill The Butcher
Yankee Phantoms

*This one's for John Fitzwilliam, who has provided me
with so much encouragement in these endeavors.*

*Photograph by the author*
The town Meeting House,
overlooking Fitzwilliam
Common, as it looks today.

# TABLE OF CONTENTS

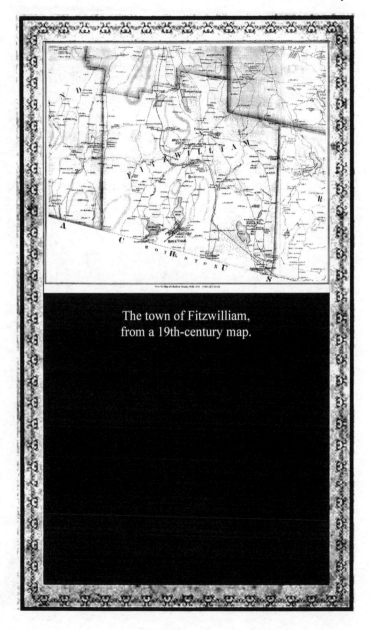

The town of Fitzwilliam,
from a 19th-century map.

# INTRODUCTION

Fitzwilliam is a sleepy little town, sitting on the intersection of Routes 12 and 119 in southern New Hampshire. It is located a scant ten miles from the Massachusetts border, where the equally quiet town of Royalston exerts its own bucolic charm. The center of this town has hardly changed from the postcards taken a century and a half ago. The Meeting House and Library still stand sentinel over the Town Common. Dexter Whittemore's old grocery store is still there, with the sign out front, although, over the years, the building has been divided into apartments. The Amos J. Blake House, home of the Fitzwilliam Historical Society, stands just across the road from the Fitzwilliam Inn, itself the source of many ghostly tales. The Fitzwilliam Tavern, however, is no more, having fallen victim to fire in the 1940s. Then there's a big old Victorian mansion on

*Photograph by the author*
Fitzwilliam Common.

the way into town, a gingerbread lady from another age. I have been told that a tenant on the second floor of this building frequently hears footsteps echoing over the ceiling above her, even though that floor is completely vacant. There are tales of British gold buried up on West Hill, and more treasure at the bottom of Laurel Lake, hidden there when it was feared that Confederate troops would overtake the town.

When I started writing this book, I approached it with some degree of trepidation. After all, would there be enough stories to justify an entire collection? Having resided here for a mere dozen years, I wouldn't presume to even think of myself as a local. But there are stories, here. Most of these tales never made it into the town histories, for various reasons. There are accounts of tragic infanticide, brutal murder, unbelievable heroism, senseless tragedy, bizarre coincidence, and even international intrigue. Not too shabby for this supposedly quiet hamlet.

The majority of these tales are taken from contemporary newspaper accounts,

WILLIAM IV.th
EARL FITZWILLIAM
BORN MAY 30 1748.
DIED FEB.y 8th 1833.

William Wentworth, Fourth
Earl of Fitzwilliam (1748-
1833), painted by William
Owen in 1817.

which, I feel, are the best source as far as getting the feel of the events at the time. On other occasions, I have cited Joel Whittemore's "History of Fitzwilliam, New Hampshire, from 1752-1887" (1888), an indispensable text for those interested in the history of the town.

Before we get to the stories, however, I think it would be a good idea to sketch over the early history of the village, so we can get a little context.

The town, originally known as Monadnock No. 4, was granted to one Roland Cotton and 41 of his associates, on January 15, 1752. Unfortunately, this group was unable to comply with the requirements of the charter, and had to forfeit the territory. Consequently, in 1765, one Samson Stoddard and 23 of his colleagues attained the land. On May 19, 1773, the residents obtained a charter from Governor Wentworth, and the town was incorporated under its present name, dubbed after William Wentworth, the Fourth Earl of Fitzwilliam. That same charter also appointed James Reed, Esq., to call the first town meeting.

*Photograph by the author*
Memorial to Brigadier General James
Reed, erected by his descendents on
Fitzwilliam Common in 1924.

Reed was one of the first really notable members of the town. Early details of his life are a little fuzzy. He was born in either Lunenburg or Woburn, Massachusetts in 1722 or 1724. In the American Revolution, he served as an officer in Colonel Brown's Massachusetts Regiment, reaching the rank of lieutenant colonel. In 1742, he married Abigail Hinds.

When news of the Battle of Lexington and Concord reached him in 1775, he gathered the local militia and marched to Boston. There, he was appointed Colonel of the Third New Hampshire Regiment, and saw action with John Stark's First New Hampshire Regiment at the Battle of Bunker Hill. On April 26, 1776, the three New Hampshire regiments were sent to help in the invasion of Canada under the command of General John Sullivan. Unfortunately, Reed only made it as far as Crown Point on Lake Champlain, whereupon he contracted smallpox, which rendered him blind and forced him to retire from military service. He was promoted to Brigadier General

Brigadier General James Reed,
painted by John E. Eckberg in 1976.
This portrait presently hangs in the
Selectman's Office.

in the Continental Army, but would never serve in that capacity due to his impaired health. He died in Fitchburg, Massachusetts, in 1807, at the age of 83. There is a monument to his memory on the Fitzwilliam Common, erected by his descendents in 1924.

The town would continue to thrive throughout the 18th and 19th centuries. As Joel Whittemore described the hamlet in his distinguished history:

"The surface of the town is broken and uneven, its lakelets, streams, hills. and valleys blending with exquisite harmony, in a landscape whose beauty is famous, and which attracts many visitors each season. Of the streams, Camp and Priest brooks, flowing a southerly course, are the largest. Among the lakelets or ponds are Rockwood and Scotts, in the northern part, and South, Meadow and Sip ponds in the southern part. Among the elevations which lend a picturesqueness to the landscape and afford delightful views, are the Pinnacle, in the central part of the town, from which may be obtained a delight-

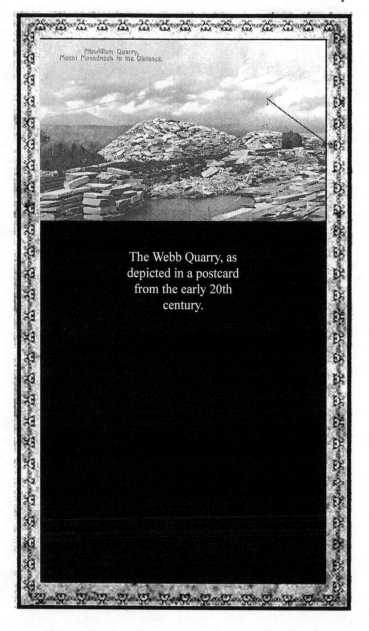

Fitzwilliam Quarry,
Mount Monadnock in the Distance.

The Webb Quarry, as
depicted in a postcard
from the early 20th
century.

ful prospect, and Gap Mountain, or Little Monadnock, lying partly in Troy, which, at a distance, appears to be a part of Monadnock. Granite of a fine quality is abundant and is extensively quarried. The soil, though rocky, is generally suitable for grazing and tillage, while there is a considerable quantity of very arable and highly productive meadow land. The original growth of timber on the uplands is maple, beech, birch, oak, pine and hemlock, and on the low lands pine, hemlock and spruce. The Cheshire railroad crosses the town in a diagonal direction from northwest to southeast."

Throughout the 18th century, the economy of the town was largely reliant on farming and the production of wooden artifacts. At one point, there were 11 sawmills within the town boundaries, turning out a huge number of kitchen and household implements. Fruit was also in abundance here, and Fitzwilliam became known as the "Blueberry Capital of the World." At this point, over a hundred bushels a day were picked by local workers, the major-

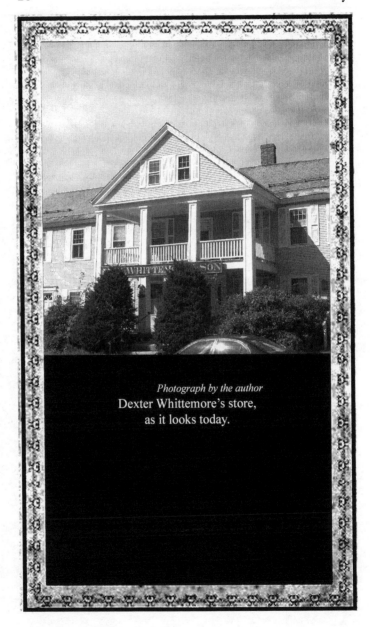

*Photograph by the author*
Dexter Whittemore's store,
as it looks today.

ity of which were shipped to Boston.

A significant business in town was the grocery store owned by Dexter Whittemore. His establishment was essentially a general goods institution — that is, until palm hats became all the rage in the mid-19th century. Beginning in 1828, Whittemore began to sell the basic supplies needed to manufacture this trendy piece of headgear. By the 1830s, he was selling 23,000 hats annually. Twenty years later, that figure shot up to 80,000. The number of hatmakers in town also mushroomed, from 250 in 1829 to more than 800 by 1860.

The introduction of the railroad altered the economy of Fitzwilliam for the next hundred years. Suddenly, the granite, which was ubiquitous, was a hot commodity, and quarries were opened up all over town. By 1886, 7,080 tons of granite were shipped out of the town in that single year. Quarries were opened up off Richmond Road, by Collins Pond, and along the Royalston Road. The largest of these were the ones operated first by Daniel Reed and subse-

The Webb Quarry, as
seen from Fitzwilliam,
from an old postcard.

quently George P. Webb of Worcester. During the apex of this industry, from 1915 to 1918, approximately 400 men were employed in the mining and processing of the stone.

By 1960, however, the demand for granite had plummeted, due largely to the popularity of cement as a building material. People began to move out of town, and seek work elsewhere. It was at this point that Fitwillam's population dropped beneath a thousand souls.

When the town's population did recover, to some extent, it was largely due to people who were working mainly in Keene, and simply lived here for the bucolic surroundings. Accordingly, it became what some would term as a "bedroom community," where the residents did most of their business elsewhere. There are a number of antique stores in town, along with a couple of restaurants and a convenience store, but not much else.

There is, however, a dark cloud on the horizon. Mining interests have begun to take notice of the vacant quarries in this town, and are determined to realize a profit from the stone that lies unclaimed on the ground. At the time of this writing, the Victoria White Quarry, which lies alongside Collins Pond Road, has already been demolished beyond recognition; additionally the Webb Quarry has been eyed for some time by the KMO Corporation.

If that weren't enough, there is also the spectre of a proposed natural gas pipeline to be erected straight through town, at the behest of the Kinder Morgan Company, of Houston, Texas.

Sorry. Had to get that off my chest, and it is possible that, by the time you read this, either or both of these situations may have already been resolved, one way or the other. Although I have resided here a scant dozen years, I feel a connection to this little town, and it really hurts to see it changed like this. One can only wonder about what the future holds, and whether Fitzwilliam's rural charm will survive the rigors of corporate greed.

Time for a few acknowledgements, I

think. First off, I have to thank Robert Corrette, a noted local historian who gave me quite a few leads to follow; additionally, Brad Decatur told me quite a few lurid stories; John Fitzwilliam led me on a few merry chases to find the strangest artifacts in the area. I am also indebted to Theresa Harlow-Sillanpaa, who is a never-ending font of fascinating local folklore. Additionally, Chelley Tighe, co-owner of the Fitzwilliam Inn, was gracious enough to show me around the house and tell me of the resident spirits. Last, but certainly not least, Alan Rumrill, of the Historical Society of Cheshire County, provided me with some ghastly accounts of the disasters that occurred on the local railroad.

I would like to make a note about my extensive use of newspaper quotes throughout this book. I wasn't trying to interject my own voice throughout the stories so much as allowing the contemporary voices to be heard. It's a bit like being a curator at a museum, and showing you around the place.

Well, that's it, really. These aren't the

Joseph E. Tardiff,
owner and operator of
Plante's store, pictured
in the early part of the
last century.

stories that you'll generally find in local histories — I realize that I've turned over a few stones in finding them. I really hope I haven't offended any relations or descendants of the parties involved by telling their stories. After all, these are tales that are meant to be told.

*Eric Stanway*
*October 31, 2015*

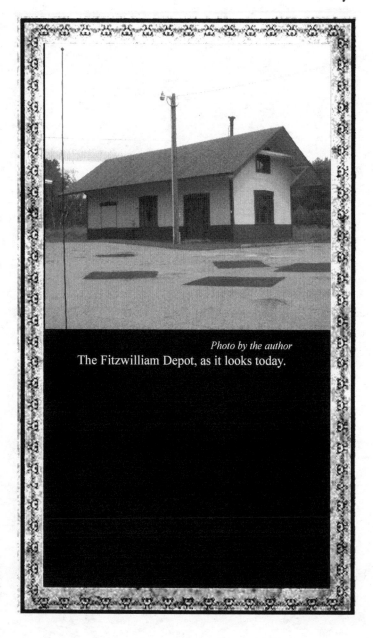

*Photo by the author*

The Fitzwilliam Depot, as it looks today.

# ONE
# THE SAD TALE OF ALFARETTA BOYCE

As I write this, it's an unseasonably cold day in May, with dark clouds rolling overhead and the roads slick with rain. Out of my window, I can see the road winding past the Fitzwilliam Depot, with the now-defunct Depot Store across the road. The atmosphere is quiet, with just the occasional car hissing down the highway, hitting the bottom of the hill, and then turning right on the route to Vermont.

This area was the scene of a desperate act, back in the biting winter of 1866, when a young girl arrived with an infant, seeking out her relatives in the hamlet of Howville, a couple of miles down East Lake Road. As she debarked the train,

The case of Caleb Boyce vs. James H. Brooks, both of Fitzwilliam, was tried Thursday and Friday. This action was brought by the plf. to recover damages ($1000 claimed) of the def. who is a minor about 18 years old, for the seduction of his daughter, Alfaretta Boyce, who was then a few days less than thirteen years old, and now about fifteen and a half years. The plf. having died since the suit was commenced, his Administrator, B. B. Boyce, came in and prosecuted the case; and because the father was dead, no damages could be recovered for the disgrace and shame brought upon the family, otherwise smart money, but only for pecuniary injury to the estate of the father in the loss of labor and money expended on account of the seduction. Verdict for the plf., damages $125. Wheeler for plf., Webster for def.

Clipping from the November 12, 1863 edition of the *New Hampshire Sentinel,* reporting on the parternity case brought against James H. Brooks by Caleb Boyce, in regards to his daughter's pregrnancy, she must have been so far deep in desperation that we could scarcely imagine the extent of her pain. She had another child five years old, and had been forced into destitution. There was no father in sight for either of them. She had a decision to make. Unfortunately, it appears that her actions were spurred by panic, leading on a trail that would find her being tried for murder.

Alfaretta Boyce was born in Fitzwilliam in 1848, the daughter of Caleb and Louisa Boyce. The first time we hear of her is some five years before the tragic events of our narrative, when her father sued a young man who had seduced her, resulting in a pregnancy, while she had yet to reach her 13th birthday. It also appears that Caleb expired before the suit reached its fruition. The whole sad story is recounted in the November 12, 1863 edition of the *New Hampshire Sentinel:*

"The case of Caleb Boyce vs. James H. Brooks, both of Fitzwilliam, was tried Thursday and Friday. This action was brought by the plaintiff to recover damages ($1000 claimed) of the defendant who is a minor about 18 years old, for the seduction of his daughter, Alfaretta Boyce, who was then a few days less than thirteen years old, and now about fifteen and a half years. The plaintiff, having died since the suit was commenced, his Administrator, R. H. Boyce, came in and prosecuted the case; and because the father was dead, no damages could be recovered for the disgrace and shame brought upon the family, otherwise smart money, but only for pecuniary injury to the estate of the father in the loss of labor and money expended on account of the seduction. Verdict for the plaintiff, damages $125. Wheeler for plaintiff, Webster for the defendant."

It would appear that the finding was far less than the family anticipated, and Alfaretta left home with her child, disappearing for the next three years.

When Alfaretta reappeared in Fitzwilliam in that frigid winter of 1866, she was literally at the end of her rope, and driven to desperate action. The *New Hampshire Sentinel* takes up the story in its March 23, 1866 edition:

"The name of this girl is Alfaretta Boyce, not quite 18 years of age. She has another illegitimate child, about 5 years old. The child killed was about four weeks old. She had brothers and sisters, and a poor, infirm mother, who was a widow. It seems that on Monday, the 5th, that bleak, cold day, with the thermometer at zero, Alfaretta got out of the cars at Fitzwilliam depot with her child in her arms, returning from a visit to a distant town, where the child was born. She immediately started on foot to Howville, a village about 3 miles distant in a southerly direction, where a number of her relatives live. She proceeded not more than 100 rods before she came to a piece of woods by the roadside. There she stopped and turned directly into the woods 8 or 10 rods, and then stripped the child of all its clothing, and put upon it a thin summer frock, tied her handkerchief firmly around its head so as to cover the mouth, that its cries might not be heard by the passers on the road; and then laid her baby down on the ground in a thicket, and left it to die!

### Infanticide in Fitzwilliam, N. H.

On Thursday, the 8th inst., the people of
Fitzwilliam, N. H., were startled at the an-
nouncement that a young girl was arraigned
before a magistrate on the charge of murder-
ing an illegitimate infant child. She plead
guilty, and was committed to Keene jail to
await the action of the Court next April. We
take the following account of the affair from
the Keene *Sentinel* :—

The name of this girl is Alfaretta Boyce, not
quite 18 years of age. She has another illegit-
emate child, about 5 years old, born when she
was but 13 years old. The child killed was
about four weeks old. She had brothers and
sisters, and a poor, infirm mother, who was a
widow. It seems that on Monday, the 5th,
that bleak, cold day, with the thermometer at
zero, Alfaretta got out of the cars at Fitzwilliam depot with her child in her arms, returning from a visit to a distant town, where the
child was born. She immediately started on
foot for Howville, a village about 3 miles distant in a southerly direction, where a number
of her relatives live. She proceeded not more
than 100 rods before she came to a piece of
woods by the roadside. There she stopped and
turned directly into the woods 8 or 10 rods, and
then stripped the child of all its clothing, and
put upon it a thin summer frock, tied her hand-

Clipping from the March 23, 1866 edition of t he
*New Hampshire Sentinel,* reporting on Alfaretta
Boyce's murder of her child.

Heart, harder the neither millstone, possessed by a girl hardly 18 years of age! — Who has the heart to plead for such a remorseless mother as this?

"She paused for a moment to gather up the little articles of dress taken from her child. The day was icy cold — the wind blew a gale — the trees creaked hard murmurs over her head. But amidst all this turmoil of nature, she thought she heard the stifling moans of her child. She became frightened, and started with frantic speed to the highway. There she picked up the things she had left, quieted her nerves for a moment, and passed on. On her arrival at Howville, she appeared cold and fatigued, but by her conduct gave no indications of the awful deed she had done.

"In a day or two it became known at Howville that she started from the depot with a child in her arms. This coming to the knowledge of her brother, he went to her and demanded an explanation of the matter. After some little hesitation, she told him the whole story. Immediately he brought her up to the selectmen

*Photo by the author*
Caleb Boyce's grave, in
the Fitzwilliam Village
Cemetery.

of Fitzwilliam village, in order to know what must be done. The first thing was to find the child. The brother and sister, with two of the selectmen, started for that purpose. On arriving at the place where she turned into the woods, she said 'stop — here is the place.' On helping her out of the buggy, she became convulsed, rigid and insensible. In a short time she came out of her fit, but vehemently exclaimed that 'she could go no further.' On much urging, she at length started with a seeming desperation, and led the way with rapid strides, directly to the spot where she had left her child. It reclined a little on one side, the limbs were slightly drawn up, and it exhibited signs of distress. It was frozen firmly to the ground, and it took some time to relieve it from its icy bed, and when it was lifted up, the leaves and moss had adhered to its side. While this was doing, Alfaretta looked on, and in a kind of musing undertone, repeated over and over again, 'I wish it was alive — I wish it was alive.'

"On coming to the village a complaint was made, and she was arraigned before a magistrate and plead guilty. But during the arraignment, although her relatives were weeping around her, she shed not a tear. And as she started for the jail she exclaimed, 'They cannot hang me too quick.' In all the conversations with her, in regard to her motives for killing her child, she merely said, she had one child, and did not want to be troubled with another."

Alfaretta was tried twice over the course of 1866. At the first, she attempted to plea guilty to second-degree murder, a motion that was rejected by the attorney general. During the second trial, however, held that November, he accepted the plea, and was found guilty in that regard. The *Keene Sentinel* commented in its November 1st edition that "the girl is no doubt below the common average of accountable beings."

Alfaretta was sentenced to an eight-year sentence in the State Prison, of which she served half. In April of 1870, she was pardoned by Governor Stearns and released.

According to local historian Robert Corrette, Alfaretta married soon after her release, and settled in Concord, where she raised a small family. He maintains she died there in 1905 or 1906, and is buried within the city limits.

There are no references to Alfaretta Boyce in the town histories, but perhaps that isn't surprising. The notoriety that she visited upon her family probably assured her an uneasy anonymity in this small town.

# THE BOSTON BUTCHERY.

## How Leavitt Alley Killed and Slaughtered Abijah Ellis.

## A SECOND WEBSTER-PARKMAN TRAGEDY.

## Interesting Details of the Trial of the Accused.

## The Evidence Circumstantial, but Terribly Convincing.

## "Father, How Came that Blood on Your Shirt?"

## THE MUTILATED CORPSE

An account of Abijah Ellis' murder, from the February 5, 1873 edition of the *New York Herald.*

# TWO

# THE BOSTON BUTCHERY

Back in 1872, some workmen at the Cambridge, Massachusetts gas works were taking a break and gazing out on the Charles River, when they noticed a strange-looking barrel floating by. On a whim, they decided to get a better look at the object, and, employing a nearby boat, brought it to shore. Upon examining the contents, however, they got a particularly ugly surprise. Inside, they were horrified to discover the hacked-up corpse of a man, his head shorn clumsily from his torso, and signs of a frenzied attack evident all over his body.

The Charles River, in
Boston, photographed
from the Back Bay, in
the 19th century.

The victim, it turned out, was one Abijah Ellis, a native of Fitzwilliam, who had traveled to Boston a quarter-century earlier, in order to seek his fortune.

Upon arriving in the city, he had bought, on credit, a load of wooden ware, which he peddled from his cart. From this inauspicious beginning, he made a sizable fortune, managing to amass enough money to enter the real estate trade. By the time of his death, his fortune was estimated to be in the vicinity of $25,000. He owned several houses in Boston, in one of which, located at 151 East Dover Street, he occupied the attic.

The problem was, Ellis was basically still a country boy at heart, with a deep distrust of banks. Consequently, he would keep sums of up to $3,000 in his pocket at any one time, which he would injudiciously exhibit to any of his companions.

It was Ellis' speculation in real estate that led directly to his demise. A teamster by the name of Leavitt Alley had recently purchased a house from him, the sum to be paid in installments. Alley was in arrears, which infuriated Ellis, as

Washington Street,
Boston, from a 19th-
century photograph.

he was a man who demanded prompt payment. It wasn't that Alley was out of pockets, either; on the Wednesday before the murder, he made a payment of $50 to another creditor

It seems that this situation reached a head in November of 1872, and the two men confronted each other in Alley's stable, located in the North End. As the argument escalated, Alley allegedly hit Ellis twice over the head with an axe, dismembered him, put him in two barrels, and deposited the remains in the Charles River.

The murder was a really big deal in Boston, and the indictment attracted a great deal of media attention. Leavitt was held without bail, and waited for trial in prison.

We can find a full account of the case in the February 5, 1873 edition of the *New York Herald*. Given the tenor of the times, it's unusually lurid in its attention to the gory details. It's also somewhat lengthy, but is worth reading, if only to get the full particulars of the case:

THE BOSTON BUTCHERY.
How Leavitt Alley Killed and
SSlaughtered Abijah Ellis.
A SECOND WEBSTER-
PARKMAN TRAGEDY.
Interesting Details of the Trial
of the Accused.
The Evidence Circumstantial,
but Terribly Convincing.
"Father, How Came that Blood on
Your Shirt?"
THE MUTILATED CORPSE
Careful Tracking of the
Alleged Assassin
IDENTIFICATION OF THE
BLOODY AXE.
Was the Victim Murdered for the
Money He Carried?

"Last November, two or three days after the general election, there was developed in this city one of the strangest and most sickening horrors that has characterized the criminal history of America for many years. Some workmen employed along the banks of the Charles River, on the Cambridge shore, discovered an old barrel floating down the stream and out to sea. A small boat being conveniently near, one of the number jumped in, and went to secure what he thought might be a prize of more or less value. Judge of the laborer's horror when he found the floating cask to contain

## THE BUTCHERED REMAINS

"of a human being. The head and legs of a man, who from all appearances had been but lately slaughtered, were here concealed in the rude barrel, and the fresh blood was scarcely through flowing from the remnants of the carcass. The features of the decapitated victim were sickening and horrible, and denoted that there had been a fearful struggle for life, and that the murderer was only successful after a desperate encounter. While the terror-stricken laborers were gazing upon the ghastly spectacle, one of their number had his attention attracted by a second barrel, similar to the one just found, floating rapidly with the tide down the same stream. To recover this was but the work of a moment, and, as may be anticipated, it contained the trunk or remaining portion of the body of him who had been so strangely and horribly slain. The cutting up had evidently been done in order that the remains could be more securely packed, and to prevent them from falling out a few slats had in each instance been nailed across the top of the casks. As before stated, everything denoted the murder was recent, the most convincing circumstance being the possession by the victim of some election ballots which had only been printed a couple of days before. In his possession was also a gold watch and chain, a pocketbook containing a sum of money and various other valuables, but still nothing to indicate who the unfortunate man was. The case, therefore, as at once

## AS MYSTERIOUS
## AS IT WAS HORRIBLE.

"It was evident that the man was not murdered for his money, and what could the motive have been? The body was given in charge of a Cambridge Coroner, and for three days was publicly exposed for identification. At the end of that time the remains were found to be those of a middle-aged and respectable man named Abijah Ellis, and belonging in Boston. The results of the efforts of the detectives cause suspicion to be directed against Leavitt Alley, a teamster, as the murderer, and in the course of a few days he was taken into custody. The evidence gathered then and since accumulated, though wholly circumstantial, is of such a nature as to leave but little doubt of the guilt of the accused, although it is possible that in the absence of direct proof he may escape conviction in the trial which has just been commenced. The case, according to the theories generally established, recalls forcibly the celebrated Webster-Parkman murder in this city some twenty odd years ago, and if the prisoner is convicted it will be upon evidence similar to that which sent Dr. Webster to the scaffold.

"The most probable solution of the affair is that Alley and Ellis had business transactions together, and the former was indebted to the latter for a considerable sum of money, which he found it difficult to provide for; that Ellis had pressed Alley for the liquidation of the debts due him; that Alley was loose and shiftless in his business habits, while Ellis was close, shrewd, economical and exacting; that the murder was committed in Alley's stable, and the body packed in some rubbish removed by him from the shop of Mr. Schouller, on Washington Street; that both Ellis and Alley were seen on Washington Street about half-past seven o'clock on the night of the murder; that outcries were heard in Alley's stable later the same evening; that Alley was seen to drive away his team, containing several barrels early the next morning, going toward the Charles river, and to return without them. There were other suspicious circumstances pointing to Alley as the man, and upon them he was accused of the murder. He received the accusation calmly and coolly, and, as Daniel Webster always advised his clients,

**HE DENIED EVERYTHING AND ADMITTED NOTHING.**

"During the two or three months of

his confinement in jail he has shrunk up quiete perceptibly — physically speaking. His appearance in court, however, does not cause one to suspect that he is the least bit nervous. Of course he manifests a lively interest in all the proceedings, but he is nevertheless as calm and serene as a Summer morning. The fact, however, that he has lost so much flesh would seem to betray something of mental anxiety. The recent harvest of murders here, as well as in New York, together with the knowledge of the profitable execution of convicted assassins in each of the cities named during the present month, has probably caused him to realize in some degree his own precarious situation.

## THE TRIAL

"of this celebrated case is of course attended with the greatest interest, and the court room and all the approaches to it have been constantly crowded during its progress. The trial is held before a special section of the Supreme Judicial court, Associate Justices Wells and

Morton on the bench. The Commonwealth is represented by Attorney General Charles R. Train and the District
Attorney for Suffolk County, John W.
May. The defendant's counsel are G.A.
Somerby, L.S. Dabney and John M. Way.
Immediately after the session of the
Court was commenced the accused was
placed at the bar for trial. The jury list
was first gone through with, and those
who had excuses to offer were allowed
to come forward and state them. The
principal excuses were from being active
members in the Ancient and Honor-
able Artillery Company, only three or
four being excused for other causes. In
selecting the panel thirty-eight jurors
were called, nineteen of whom were
challenged by the defendant, four by
the government and three were excused,
having formed opinions as to the guilt of
the prisoner. As finally selected, the jury
was composed of the following gentlemen: — Nelson C. Hazelton (foreman),
Samuel Ashman, Henry Edwell, Jr.,
William B. Fenner, Frederick Folsom,

John M. Humphrey, Thomas King, Benjamin F. Mahan, George Morse, Charles F. Morgan, Nathaniel M. Nason and Ira A. Nay, to communicate with their families by message, as they will be kept together during the trial.

## THE INDICTMENT

"was then read amid a most painful silence. It contains four counts, the first alleging that Alley killed Ellis with an axe; the second alleges the killing to have been done with a club; the third charges that the murder was committed by choking and strangling, and the fourth count by means to the jurors unknown. (The last count was drawn to meet an objection which arose in the Webster-Parkman case.) After the reading of the indictment had bee concluded the Clerk said: — 'To this indictment, gentlemen of the jury, the prisoner has pleaded 'Not guilty,' and for the trail has put himself upon the country, which country you are. You are sworn to try the issue. If he is guilty you are to say so; if he is not guilty you are to say so and no more.

Good men and true, stand together and hearken to the evidence.'

### THE SUPPOSED SCENE OF THE MURDER VISITED BY THE JURY.

"Attorney General Train then addressed the Court, and stated that before the case was opened for the government it was desirable that the jury should visit the premises where the deed was committed. Mr. Somerby, counsel for the defendant, made no opposition to proposition of the Attorney General, but also desired that the jury might visit Alley's house in Metropolitan place, as it might become important during the trial. To this request the Attorney General acceded, and the Court granted the motions. The jury, in charge of Sheriff Clark and Deputies Hayley and Goodwin, accompanied by District Attorney May for the government and G.A. Somerby for the defendant, left the court room and took carriages for Alley's stable, at the corner of Hunneman and Fellows streets, his house on Metropolitan place and his team stand on Washington Street.

## WHAT THE GOVERNMENT PROPOSES TO PROVE.

"District Attorney May, in opening the case for the government, after alluding to the importance of the trial, proceeded to intimate what the government evidence would establish. When the several portions of the body were discovered, he said, a thorough examination was made, but nothing was found at that time to furnish a clew, until in one of the barrels was discovered a piece of brown paper with the name of 'P. Schouller, No. 1,049 Washington street.' Naturally the clew tended toward Mr. Schouller, and investigation proved that Mr. Alley had been in the habit of removing shavings from Mr. Schouller's billiard manufactory to his stable on Hunneman street. Following the clew to Mr. Alley's stable, it was found a dry manure heap had been recently been disturbed. An examination of some boards behind the manure heap disclosed that there were

Harrison Avenue,
Boston, photographed in
the 19th century.

## HUNDREDS OF DROPS
## OF BLOOD

"upon them, varying from little spots to those of much larger size. The government would show that these spots were blood as certain as science can demonstrate. It would be shown that on the Monday night previous three barrels of shaving were taken from Mr. Schouller's to Alley's stable, and that in one of these barrels was found to contain the head of Mr. Ellis. It would be shown that on Tuesday night one of these barrels was emptied by Mr. Alley and locked up by him. Mr. Alley took the key home in his pocket, and as near as can be ascertained, even by the prisoner's own statement, he arrived as his stable a few minutes before five o'clock the next morning, and found everything in its usual condition. At a quarter past six o'clock, Mr. Alley was called upon by a man who wanted him to do a job. Soon after Mr. Alley's son and a Mr. Tibbetts, employed by Mr. Alley, arrived at the stable. About twenty minutes before seven an express wagon

The North End, Boston,
from a 19th-century
photograph.

large enough to contain four barrels was hitched to an old black horse always driven by Mr. Alley and he started for Washington street. As he was about starting the man who had engaged him to do a job at eleven o'clock jumped upon the wagon and turned up one of the barrels, which was lying upon the blige. Mr. Alley said to him,

### IF YOU WANT TO RIDE WITH ME, COME FORWARD.

"The man started to do so, but just then the horse started, and in the effort to save himself the man caught onto another barrel, and on lifting it found there was something in it. Mr. Alley then drove to his house, on Metropolitan place, near Riscten's stable, where he left two empty barrels. At half-past seven o'clock a party driving past the rail dam met, about two hundred feet from the sluiceway, an express wagon, with an old black horse, so grievously afflicted with the horse disease as to attract attention. The driver of the wagon he did not notice particularly, but the view he had of him nowise differs from the description of the prisoner. In the wagon the party noticed two barrels, lying side by side, covered with a piece of green carpet. Subsequently this man, at the stable of Alley, overhauled a lot of bagging and other materials, and identified the piece of green carpet which he had seen covering the barrels in Alley's wagon. On the day the man met Alley on the milldam he was proceeding in the direction of Parker street, and when about to turn up that street he looked around and saw Alley with an empty team going in the direction of Boston.

### THE BARRELS WERE NOWHERE TO BE SEEN,

"and the government would claim that the barrels were thrown into the sluiceway by Leavitt Alley and that they afterward floated up to Cambridge, where they were found. As to the mode and manner in which Abijah Ellis came to his death there was no absolute certainty, but that it was by violence there could be no doubt. Mr. Ellis lodged at

No. 151 East Dover street."

(As an aside, it is interesting to note that East Dover Street was notorious for its brothels and saloons. As a matter of fact, the area developed such an unsavory reputation that the name of the street was changed to East Berkely street, although the Dover elevated railway line remained there until the late 1980s. The author can personally attest to the dangerous atmosphere that this street held, as he walked it many times. At the time of this writing, there is presently a movement among local residents to have the original name restored.)

"The last time he was seen or heard of was about five o'clock on Tuesday morning (election day). About twelve o'clock he was known to have inquired for Mr. Alley, and the jury would be satisfied that Mr. Alley had agreed to meet Mr. Ellis at two o'clock and to pay him some money. Mr. Ellis took his meals at No. 3 Smith avenue, near Hammond Park. He was last seen alive about seven o'clock that evening when he left that place. Mr. Alley

East Berkely Street, formerly East Dover Street, photographed in 1986. The Dover Street Station, pictured here, has since been demolished.

left his house at about the same hour, and his course would naturally be the same as Mr. Ellis', who was returning to his lodgings. How they met and what transpired was known only to Abijah Ellis and to God. Within two hours after Mr. Ellis took his supper he was dead, and in all human probability

## HIS CORPSE WAS
## HACKED TO PIECES

"and placed in the barrels where they were found. According to Mr. Alley's statement he locked his stable about seven o'clock that night and unlocked it about five o'clock the next morning. The government would show the jury that on the night of election, between seven and nine o'clock, an altercation took place in that stable, and that sounds of a human voice was heard and a noise as if barrels were being rolled. The next morning, it would appear that Alley's son said to him: — 'Father, how came that blood on your shirt bosom!'

"He replied: — 'It came from the nostrils of a horse.' Upon examination of his clothing shortly after by the Chief of Police there was no blood upon the shirt, and Alley denied having changed it.

"Mr. May then described with much earnestness the fearful wounds made upon the head of Mr. Ellis, and from all appearances that the blow was inflicted by a muscular person from behind the victim, and was intended to launch him into eternity. An axe was a fearful thing n this case to the defendant, whoever it might be. When asked if he had bought an axe Mr. Alley replied in the negative; but it would be shown that on the 31st of October he purchased a new axe, which was seen in the stable only a day or two before the murder. If Mr. Alley was not the party who was seen at the various points mentioned then it was some person who bore a strong resemblance to him; but, when all the circumstances were taken into consideration, the finger of guilt pointed strongly to Leavitt Alley.

### THE TESTIMONY.

"The witnesses for the government

were then called and sworn and the witnesses on both sides were excluded from the court room on motion of the Attorney General, ther defense objecting thereto.

### THE FINDING OF THE BODY.

"Stephen McFadden was the first witness called. I reside in Cambridgeport; on the 6th of November, at three o'clock or quarter-past, I saw a barrel floating up the river; I took a boat and went out for it and discovered a dead man in it; when I first saw the barrel only a part of the bottom was visible; the barrel only had one head; after the body was taken ashore it was given in charge of two constables; nothing was taken out of the barrel before the arrival of the constables; there was horse manure in the barrel; it contained the shoulders, arms and thighs of a man; later in the afternoon I discovered another barrel floating toward Boston; this was about half an hour after the first one was seen; I assisted in getting it ashore, and it contained the head, legs and hat of a man.

(A hat was here shown witness, who said it looked like the one he saw in the barrel. The barrels were also brought into Court, and the witness identified the larger one as the one found by him in the river.) There was found in the man's pockets some keys, nails and a pencil, and when the body was carried into the shed a gold watch was found on the ground where he lay.

"Several Cambridge police officers here testified to seeing the body in the barrels and to taking charge of the same and delivering it to the Cambridge Coroner.

## THE BARREL AND
## THE SHAVINGS.

"Peter Schouller, the next witness, testified as follows: — 'My business is the manufacture of billiard tables at 1,049 Washington street, where I have been for about five years. (Witness was then shown a piece of brown paper bearing his name, which he said he threw into the shavings.) The last time had had seen the paper before to-day was when he was at the Coroner's hearing in Cambridge; the shavings in my shop were all taken away by Leavitt Alley since the 30th of March last; sometimes Alley would take them away once a week, and then not for a fortnight; about six o'clock on Monday afternoon, the day before election, Alley took away three barrels of shavings, which I helped him pack; one barrel was larger than the others; I did not see Alley on the day of election, but the morning after, between eight and nine o'clock he came into the shop; I did not see him at any other time that morning; the larger barrel of the two in the court room I saw in my shop on Monday evening, November 4; it belonged to Alley. Mr. Schouller then examined the shavings in the larger barrel and said they were pine and black walnut, the same as were in his shop.

"Cross-examined — Don't know any more about these barrels than I did at Cambridge; I did not say at Cambridge that these are the same barrels, but I did say that the shavings in the larger barrels were wet while at Cambridge; I would not swear that I ever saw either of these barrels in my shop; can't swear that the shavings came from my shop; I can't read English and don't know what the writing was on the paper shown to me by Mr. May; I am sure, however that it came from my shop as no other person in Boston has them; children and others used to get shavings as well as Mr. Alley; a month or so before election day Alley dumped shavings upon a heap outside the shop; never objected to anybody taking shavings; the large barrel I saw in Cambridge I think was not so large as the one I saw in my shop; Mr. Kimball, who worked for me, has had shavings once in every two or three months for four years past; a colored man used to come and get the shavings for Kimball; when shown some moulding at Cambridge, I said I hadn't repaired anything of that kind for over a year, and I still say so; at Cambridge I was shown some pieces of wood which were never in my shop; when parties came to my shop for shavings I would let them have any barrel there was lying around.

"Redirect — The last time Mr. Kimball or the colored man took shavings from my shop was on Saturday or Monday before election; they took away one or two barrels, but not any barrels belonging to Alley; Alley got more shavings than anybody else. Mr. Schouller was then shown a piece of moulding which was taken from the larger barrel, and he said that he had some of that kind of moulding which was taken from the larger barrel, and he said that he had some of that kind of moulding in the upper part of his shop, but had not used any of it for a year.

## THE WALNUT CHIPS.

"Michael Schouller, a son of the last witness, testified that pine, chestnut and black walnut were mostly used at his father's establishment; Mr. Alley used to take shavings away in barrels of his own; they were, as I understood Mr. Alley, used as bedding; the rubbing in the shop, such as was not fit for bedding, Mr. Alley dumped; occasionally children took away shavings, and on the Monday before election Mr. Kimball had two barrels; last saw Mr. Alley in my shop on the Thursday after election; on Wednesday saw him there in the neighborhood of eight o'clock, when witness gave him directions to go down town and get tools for one of his workmen; I did not know Mr. Abijah Ellis; cannot tell how many barrels of shavings Alley took away Tuesday, whether it was three or more or less. The witness was then shown the brown paper which was previously alluded to, and said that on the 18th of October he paid a bill of $31 to an express man; paid a bill of a like amount on the 30th of August; these amounts were marked on the outside of the wrapper, C.O.D.; after the packages were opened the wrappers were thrown among the shavings.

"On cross-examination Mr. Schouller said he didn't remember whether or not on the day of election he had promised to pay Mr. Alley a bill of about thirty dollars when he should have carried the billiard table away; at Cambridge I saw some pieces of wood, which I said didn't come from my place; also saw a piece of a pocket from a billiard table, which I said couldn't have come from my place for three months prior.

"Redirect — I don't remember having any conversation about money with Alley on Tuesday, election day, nor do I think I paid him any money on Wednesday.

"Mr. May then proposed to show to the jury the piece of brown wrapping paper found among the shavings of one of the barrels, and also Mr. Schouller's bills of $31 each (the same as marked on the brown paper), bearing date of August 30 and October 18 respectively.

"Mr. Somerby objected to having bills shown the jury, on the ground that they had nothing to do with the identification of the shavings. The District Attorney abandoned his proposition to offer the bills, and the brown paper was only submitted to the jury.

### TESTIMONY OF ALLEY'S TEAMSTER.

"John Tebbetts was the next witness,

testifying as follows: — Am twenty years old, and have lived in Boston since last June; came from Ohio, a town adjoining one where Alley lived; have worked for him since in Boston; drove a team; he had four horses; one was red, with black mane and tail; the one he drove was an old black horse; in November the black horse had the horse disease; at that time the stable was divided into stalls and grain and hay bins; witness described the interior of the stable by a plan which was produced, and pointed out different parts of it; the barrels were exhibited; don't remember that I ever saw these barrels before; they are common barrels anyway; I went to Mr. Schouller's for shavings on the evening of the election day; took away three barrels; two of them were floor barrels and the other a larger barrel; took them away about six o'clock, and carried them to Alley's stable, on Hunneman Street.; the shavings were such as would be made in billiard table work; one of the barrels, the large one, was emptied under one horse and another under another horse; this was done a little after six; the horses were fed and the stable locked; he then went into the house; don't know

### WHO LOCKED THE DOORS;

"there were five carriages belonging to Alley and carriage belonging to Mr. Kelley, in the stable; witness described the carriages; after I got home washed and ate my supper; think Mr. Alley went out; at the table Curtis Alley said he had left out a stove down at the stand, and Mr. Alley said he would go down and take it in, as it was raining; it was then near eight o'clock, I think; didn't see Mr. Alley that night again; I went to the stable about six o'clock next morning. Mr. Alley and a Mr. Baker were there; Mr. Alley had hold of his black horse at the door of the stable; the horse was in good condition as to flesh, but not poor or very fat; Curtis Alley went with me; been fed when we got there; that morning the wagon Alley usually drove was there, and had two barrels in it; they were partly covered up with a horse blanket; they were lying lengthwise of the wagon; could not see whether they were dark or light; was not there when Alley left; I took a horse to get shod; when I returned Alley was gone; I then went down to the stand where Curtis Alley was; soon after took a load of wood from Harrison Avenue and drove to Hyde Park; didn't come in sight of the stand again before noon; as I passed Metropolitan place there was no team there; in the stable there was a manure heap, quite large; the pile was about two feet high; saw the board near the manure heap on Saturday morning after election

### WITH BLOOD ON THEM;

"these are the boards to the stall where my horse stood; the shavings were piled upon the manure heap; on Wednesday morning saw some blood on Alley's shirt, and Curtis asked his father where the blood came from; he said it came from a horse he had struck; his bosom was spattered with blood; saw no indications of a horse having been struck, or blood on any horse; he didn't say which horse; made no particular examination of the horses; on Thursday evening the subject of finding a body in the Charles River was discussed by Alley's family; Alley said he had better put down in writing where we were on Tuesday evening, as the discovery of the shavings, billiard pockets, barrels & c., might make it go hard on me (horse blanket shown); recognize this blanket as the one used by Alley to cover the barrels on his wagon; don't know whether the manure heap was the same on Wednesday morning as on Tuesday night; I worked for Alley from the 7th of August to the 9th of November; on the Saturday before election. Curtis Alley

## ASKED HIS FATHER
## FOR MONEY

"for me; he replied that he couldn't let me have any, as he had paid $50 on his house that day; didn't succeed in getting any; the memorandum I made as to my whereabouts on Tuesday was given to the Chief of Police; there was a new light axe in Mr. Alley's stable; I call it red in color; saw it Monday before election; we used it that day. (Axe shown.) This is not the axe, but I may have seen this before; have not seen the red axe since; looked after it on the Friday morning after election, but couldn't find it; Thursday after election it rained hard; one of the teams went out at about three P.M. but none before; don't know that Alley had any business with Ellis, except what I heard him say; he said he paid him $50 on the house; had seem them together a few days before election; only saw them talking together in the stable rear of Ristan's store; don't know what they were talking about; they appeared to be on good terms; saw Ellis once on the Monday before election on Shawmut avenue; Ellis was walking and Alley and I were on a team; have seen Ellis at the stand when he had inquired for Alley; the barrels in Alley's wagon had heads in them in the ends towards me; didn't see Alley after I left him Wednesday morning until the evening; never saw any other

## NEW AXE IN THE STABLE;

"there was an old one which Alley said was stolen several days before. The further direct examination of this witness was suspended until the memorandum made by him could be found,

"Cross-examined — Left the stable election night about six o'clock and went to the house; about the time Alley went out I went to bed; when I got to the stable the next morning I helped get out the wagons, and then led a lame horse to the blacksmith shop half a mile from the stable; can't tell how long a time it took to do all this; don't know what time Alley took his breakfast that morning; can't fix the time I arrived at the stand, but think it was about seven o'clock; Mr. Alley, Curtis and I had keys to the stable; Mr. Kelley had a key to the stable some time before.

"Redirect — Heard nothing said in Alley's hearing in regard to fixing the time of his coming home on election night.

## AN IMPORTANT WITNESS

"Ellen Kelly testified — Live in

Spring Court, No. 6, close to Alley's stable; the house and stable are separated only by a small alleyway; remember election day evening; went through the alleyway to a store; think it was about seven o'clock; there was a noise and men talking in the stable when I was going out; when I returned I heard a man say 'God d—n you;' there was a light in the stable, which was burning until ten o'clock, when I went to bed; went out a second time to get a pail of water; heard talking in the stable and a noise like the rolling of barrels.

"Cross-examined — This was on election night; can't tell who was voted for that day, as women don't bother themselves about such things; didn't notice much about the talk and rolling of barrels in the stable; first told this story to a man who came to see me on Friday night; don't know who he was, but I'll tell you he was eating peanuts; told it two or three times; an officer told me not to tell anymore about it.

**THE CORONER'S STORY.**

"Dr. W.W. Wellington testified: —

Am a physician and Coroner in Cambridge; held an inquest on the remains of Abijah Ellis; it was commenced on the 6th of November last and continued several days; sessions were held on the 7th, 8th, 9th, 10th, 11th, 12th and 19th of November; saw two barrels, which, I think, are the ones shown here; first saw them on Wednesday, the 5th of November; was called to the gas works and saw the trunk, arms and part of the legs of a human body; a barrel, with a head and legs, was brought in afterwards; there were some shavings and rubbish in the barrels also; I took possession of several articles found in the pockets; founds a bunch of keys, two copper nails, a piece of scrip and a lead pencil; since turned them over to the executor of Mr. Ellis; the remains had on a dark suit, dirty, and an old hat; the hat shown is like the one found; the legs of the pants were cut and correspond with the cut on the human legs; witness examined the clothing and identified them as the same; the boots were cut off; the clothing was given to the police of Cambridge and shown at the inquest; it was given to the Boston officers and a receipt taken; a list of the articles given to Detectives Wood and Dearborn was read; the clothing was taken from the remains in my presence and by my order.

"Cross-examined — A man brought in a watch which, he said, was found on the body; the watch was stopped at eleven o'clock; when I arrived at the gas works there were 100 persons there; the remains were out of the first barrel and on the ground; they were carried to a shed and then a second barrel was brought in; all the pockets were searched in my presence; never knew or saw Abijah Ellis; gave the watch found to J.Q.A. Bracket, the executor.

## DAMAGING TESTIMONY.

"Franklin A. Ramsell testified: — I reside on Park street, Highlands; am a teamster; have driven for Mergurie & Co.; on Wednesday after the election I got up, harnessed my horse and came to the city by the Brookline avenue; the bell was ringing as I got on my team on

the way in; I met a team with two barrels on it; when I got to Parker street
the team passed me again without the
barrels; I looked on the wagon and saw
they were gone; looked up the milldam
and couldn't see them; the horse had
epizootic very badly which called my
attention to it; didn't notice the driver
particularly; the driver was a short, stout
man; can't remember how he looked or
was dressed; the wagon was a common
furniture wagon; didn't notice the name
on it; the barrels were mostly covered up;
could see the heads and hoops of one;
did not notice the size; one barrel was
new and the other old and black; they
were covered with an old carpet; have
seen one piece of carpet since which
resembled it in Alley's stables; found it
in a pile of carpets in a stall; there were
a number of pieces in the pile, which I
pulled over before I found the piece; I
thought it was the one seen on the barrels; it was on Saturday after the election
that I found the carpet; saw a wagon at
the stable, but I can't say if it was the

—The Funeral of Abijah Ellis, who was brutally murdered in Boston a week ago, occured in Fitzwilliam, on Tuesday last in the Orthodox church in that town. There were several of his old friends in that town present. The sermon was preached by Rev. Mr. Day, and was a very impressive discourse. The pallbearers were Messrs. Milton Chaplin, an old business associate of Mr. Ellis, Chauncy Davis, Leonard Byam and Banister Pratt, all acquaintances of his boyhood. The remains were deposited in a rosewood casket, music was furnished by the church choir, and the remains of the unfortunate man were interred in the town burying ground

A clipping from the
November 20, 1872 edition
of the *Farmer's Cabinet,*
reporting on the funeral of
Abiijah Ellis.

one I saw near the milldam; saw a horse there which looked like the one seen; he was a black horse, very poor, and had the disease very bad; don't remember that I gave the piece of carpet found at the stable to anyone after recognizing it; (piece shown) this doesn't look like the one I found.

"An attempt was made to show that witness had described the barrels before the Coroner b asking him he did not there describe them.

"Before the Coroner I said that the old barrel was not all covered, but the new one was covered, so that only the head could be seen; explained to the Coroner that by the large barrel I meant the old barrel; think the bell I heard ring before testified to was the bell I hear every morning; when I met the wagon on the mill dam it was 200 feet from the sluiceway and about a thousand feet from where I was on the corner of Parker street; the piece of carpet shown here doesn't look like the one I picked up from the pile at the stable.

"Cross-examined — It is a mile from my house down to the mill dam; the horse in the strange team was very poor and thin; the tide runs through the sluiceway for half an hour after the tide turns and runs up.

## ALLEY SEEN ON CHARLES STREET.

"Mr. W.S. Richards testified: — I live in Newton, Highlands, and do business in Bedford street, Boston; at the time of the November election I lived on Chandler street; on Wednesday morning I saw Leavitt Alley between Charles and Beacon streets; I think he was driving a dark bay horse; he was driving slowly; it was between seven and eight o'clock in the morning when I saw him; I was on my way to my stable, in Ashton place, when I saw Alley; my business is that of an express man; don't remember seeing him on any other day of the week; Wednesday was a pleasant day; after I saw Alley I saw my men and Mr. Baxter; the latter I met on Bedford street, and went down to market with him; don't remember going with Baxter on any other day of the week; between seven and eight o'clock on election day I was somewhere between Chandler and Bedford streets; one of my horses was sick, and I didn't drive him on Monday or Tuesday; on Wednesday I used him, and drove Captain Baxter with him."

There is more, but at this point, it just gets repetitive. What is astonishing about this case is that, even with the sheer number of witnesses willing to attest to Alley's guilt, he was acquitted. Although the evidence was circumstantial, it was also extremely damning. One would suspect that, given modern forensic medicine, Alley's goose would be cooked. As it was, however, the science of the time was unable to distinguish between human blood and that of an animal. For instance, we have this account from the Middletown, Connecticut *Constitution*, from their February 19 edition:

"The trial of Leavitt Alley for the murder of Abijah Ellis, which has been progressing in Boston for some weeks, and has closed in a verdict of not guilty, stands among one of the more remarkable cases of the age…

"…Blood was found on Alley's clothing, and every link in the chain seemed strong enough to fasten the net upon him.

"But as the trial progressed the case of Alley improved. It was shown that a horse had been bled in the stable a few days previous, and experts were set at examining the blood clots. The doctors disagreed — as usual. One averred that the blood was from a human body, and further from Ellis's body. Another as strongly asserted that it was simply the blood of a horse, but others testified that it was impossible to tell the difference between human and animal blood after it has dried. What could the jury do but discard this important part of the case of the state? Then it was shown that Alley had a comfortable sum of money in the bank, and was not hard pressed by Ellis; that on the night of the murder he had been paid a debt by his son, thus accounting for his flush pocketbook the next day; and more important still, the defense satisfactorily accounted for Alley's whereabouts from the moment Ellis disappeared to the time of his murder. On these grounds the jury's duty seemed plain, and a verdict of acquittal was quickly rendered. And the murder remains as mysterious as before."

Although Leavitt Alley walked a free man, his victory did not last long. He died a mere three years later, a shroud of suspicion still clinging to hm.

And what of poor Abijah Ellis? His mangled remains were brought back to Fitzwilliam, for a decent interment. We have this account from the November 20, 1872 edition of the *Farmer's Cabinet:*

"The Funeral of Abijah Ellis, who was brutally murdered in Boston a week ago, occurred in Fitzwilliam, on Tuesday last in the Orthodox church in that town. There were several of his old friends in that town present. The sermon was preached by Rev. Mr. Day, and was a

*Photo by the author*
Abijah Ellis' grave, in
the Fitzwilliam Village
Cemetery.

very impressive discourse. The pallbearers were Messrs. Milton Chaplin, an old business associate of Mr. Ellis, Chauncy Davis, Leonard Byam and Banister Pratt, all acquaintances of his boyhood. The remains were deposited in a rosewood casket, music was furnished by the church choir, and the remains of the unfortunate man were interred in the town burial ground."

It is doubtful that Abijah Ellis rests easily in his grave. Well, nobody should fault him for feeling a certain sense of injustice. As no other parties were arrested or indicted in the murder, it remains technically unsolved to this day. Without a doubt, this stands as one of the ghastliest cases to be associated with the fair town of Fitzwilliam.

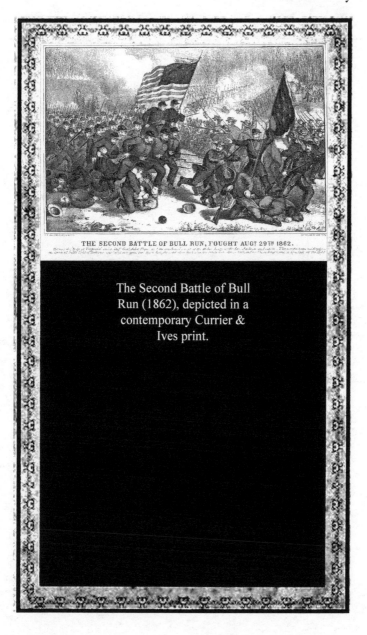

THE SECOND BATTLE OF BULL RUN, FOUGHT AUGT 29TH 1862.

The Second Battle of Bull Run (1862), depicted in a contemporary Currier & Ives print.

# THREE
# SIX NIGHTS
# ON THE FIELD

There's a lot to be said for the resilience of the human spirit. There are tales of those who have prevailed, lost out at sea, tangled in the jungle, or wandering the desert. Of course, there are some whose sheer will to live against overwhelming odds fills us all with a sense of admiration for their sheer courage.

Certainly, Fitzwilliam native William Dunton falls into this category. What he went through would have broken a lesser man's mind and body. Basically, Dunton was one tough old hunk of New England granite.

Dunton was born on May 24, 1824,

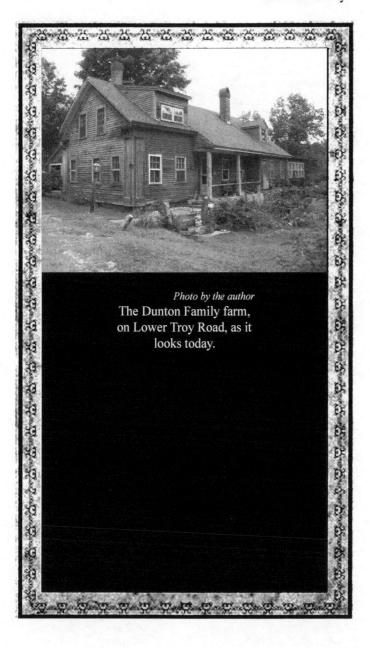

*Photo by the author*
The Dunton Family farm,
on Lower Troy Road, as it
looks today.

to Abel Dunton and Ruth A. Phillips. His grandfather, James Dunton, was one of the original settlers of Fitzwilliam, having moved here from Southboro, Massachusetts.

Over a period of 20 years, Dunton manufactured woodenware for N. & J. Howe, a concern operating out of Howville. In 1861, he abandoned this trade, and was first in line to enlist in the fight for the Union. He was assigned to the Second New Hampshire Volunteers. We have this account of this regiment's departure from the May 2, 1861 edition of the *New Hampshire Sentinel:*

"SEE TO OUR SOLDIERS — We learn from a gentleman just returned from Concord, that the company which left Keene last week arrived there in good spirits and were gladly received, they being the second company that pre-sented themselves at head quarters, and are styled 'Company B' — We also learn that they are now in rather a destitute condition for underclothes, not having carried a change, which they should

The aftermath of the
Second Battle of Bull
Run, as photographed by
Matthew Brady.

have done. The ladies of Keene will send to Concord such articles as our soldiers will need, and if those in the neighboring towns who have friends in the company at Concord, will send clothing to Keene, such as shirts, drawers, stockings, shoes, and pants, they will be forwarded to them immediately. All bundles must be marked to whom they are to be sent and left with Capt. H.C. Handerson, Recruiting officer at Keene."

It didn't take Dunton long to find himself in the thick of the fighting. He saw action in Virginia in 1861 and 1862. He prevailed through various campaigns including the First Battle of Bull Run and sorties on the Virginia Peninsula, from Williamsburg to Harrison's Landing, and remained pretty much unscathed. However, at the Second Battle of Bull Run, on August 29, 1862, his luck ran out. He was shot in the face, and spent the next six days on the field, hideously wounded, before being rescued by Union troops. For a full account of the man's ordeal, we turn to "The His-

*Photo by the author*
Abel Dunton's grave, in
the Fitzwilliam Village
Cemetery.

tory of Fitzwilliam, From 1752 to 1787," by John Foote Nelson and Joel Whittemore (1888):

"…[I]n the second Bull Run fight, he was struck by a ball on the right cheek, which, passing through his mouth so as to break up the bone and teeth of the entire upper jaw, came out just below the eye on the left cheek. Mr. Dunton fell, and was left by his comrades as dead, when, shortly after, they were obliged to retreat. Being now a. prisoner, he was stripped of nearly all his clothes and of almost everything he had by the enemy, and left to die. Finding his mouth and throat fast filling up from the swelling of the mangled flesh, he succeeded in getting his knife from his pocket and deliberately cut away the torn flesh, and so cleared his mouth as far as possible.

"Hours now passed, and so did nights and days, and no relief was at hand. He could not cry out or even speak aloud, and could not have swallowed a morsel of food or a drop of water if he had had either.

"For six days and nights he endured

what must have been agony, but on the morning of the seventh day he was discovered by a party of our own men who were burying the dead. He was still alive, but so weak that the men at first despaired of his living till he could be removed to a hospital. Faint and exhausted he was at length placed in the hands of the surgeons at Washington, five of whom decided that no human skill could save him. Still, desiring to give him a chance for recovery, they dressed his wounds, inserted a small tube in his throat, and finally succeeded in having him swallow a few drops of brandy, which revived him. Mr. Dunton was fed in this way for more than a month, and still lives, after more than twenty years, to tell the story of his sufferings, and to remind all who meet him of the enormous cost involved in saving our country."

It is said that, upon returning to Fitzwilliam, Dunton would frequent the Fitzwilliam Inn, where he would tell the tale of how he lost about half of his face to anyone who would listen.

In 1871, William Dunton took over the farm and lands from his father for a token exchange of $1, and bond. Thus, he resumed his trade as a farmer. Abel continued to live on the property, expiring on April 21, 1882.

Horrible as Dunton's disfigurement was, it did not bar him from matrimony. As a matter of fact, he married late in life. The *New Hampshire Sentinel* reported on January 30, 1889, as follows:

"On Sunday, William Dunton was married to Mrs. (Mary A. Richardson) Hayden. We wish them more joy than the very stormy day portended for them."

Dunton continued to work on the farm, putting in much more work than might be expected of a man of his advanced years and violent history. This, however, was not without its mishaps. We have this account of one such accident reported in the July 9, 1890 edition of the *New Hampshire Sentinel:*

"William Dunton was thrown from a load of hay last week and severely lamed and bruised, and though he is

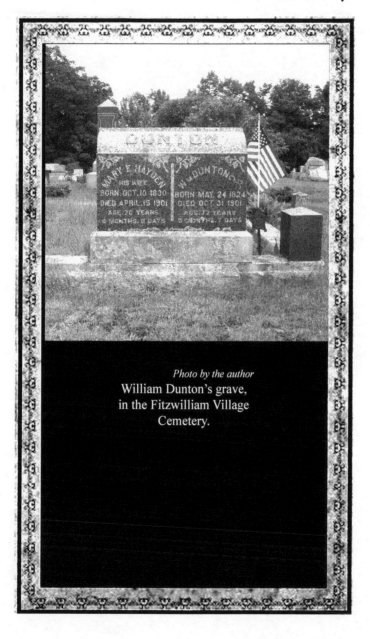

*Photo by the author*
William Dunton's grave,
in the Fitzwilliam Village
Cemetery.

able to sit up only a short time as yet, it is hoped he will be about soon."

Actually, Dunton lived for eleven more years, amazing locals with the tale of his incredible ordeal. When his wife passed away on April 15 of 1901, however, he no doubt decided that his life had run its course. On Halloween of that year, he decided to end it all, committing suicide by gunshot.

Despite this sad ending, however, we still have reason to be astonished by this man's courage and resilience in the face of overwhelming odds. William Dunton was a true son of New Hampshire, hard as granite, and resilient to the core.

# WHO'S BEST FIDDLER?
# MURDER ENDS
# DISPUTE

---

Poles, Under Influence of Liquor in
Lumber Camps, Quarrel Over
Their Respective Merits as Vir-
tuosi—Murderer Under Arrest.

---

Keene, N H, Aug 1—Vaschi Czen-
osos, a Pole who was arrested tod:y
at a lumber camp near Fitzwill'am,
chuiged with killing a fellow-countrv-
man, Adam Carpiska, after a quarrel

Clip from the August 2,
1906 edition of *The Boston
Journal,* reporting on the
murder of Adam Carpisca.

# FOUR
# A DISHARMONIOUS EVENING

**M**usicians can be touchy people. Most of the time, they're pretty proud of their skills, and take umbrage at anyone who might question them. Generally, however, this just leads to a bout of inspired playing; rarely does it lead to violence.

On one hot night in July of 1906, however, that is exactly what happened. The tragedy unfolded in Fitzwilliam, resulting in hot-blooded murder, and further culminated in the brutal killing of an innocent woman on the shores of Canobie Lake.

As our story opens, two Polish woodcutters, Vaschi Czenovos and Adam Carpisca, were finishing off their day in the Fitzwilliam lumberyards by imbibing liberal quantities of whiskey and playing the fiddle. Some time during the evening, the question came up as to which was the better musician. Well, things got a little out of hand, and Carpisca decided to bash Czenovos over the head with his instrument. He then went to a shed on the property to sleep it off.

Apparently, this fight wasn't over as far as Czenovos was concerned. As he sat and drank more whisky, his mood grew darker and darker. Finally, he decided to follow Carpisca out, and exact brutal revenge. The tragic turn of events is chronicled in the following piece from the August 2, 1906 edition of *The Boston Journal:*

### WHO'S BEST FIDDLER? MURDER ENDS DISPUTE

*Poles, Under Influence of Liquor in Lumber Camps, Quarrel Over Their Respective Merits as Virtuosi — Murderer Under Arrest.*

"Keene, N.H. Aug. 1 — Vaschi Czenovos, a Pole who was arrested today at a lumber camp near Fitzwilliam, charged with killing a fellow-countryman Adam

Carpiska *[sic]* after a quarrel last night, was held without bail this afternoon for the October session of the Superior Court. A dispute over their abilities as fiddlers is said to have led to the killing. The lumbermen in the camp where the two men were employed were paid off by the contractor yesterday, and some of them had a celebration last evening, during which they drank whisky. Czenovos and Carpiska each played the violin and became angry over the question of which was the better player. Carpiska is said to have broken a violin over the head of his rival, after which he went out of the camp, and going under a shed, fell asleep there.

"According to the testimony of witnesses at the hearing this afternoon in Justice Holmes' court, Czenovos followed Carpiska out of the house and struck him over the head with a heavy club as he lay under the shed. Afterward Czenovos is said to have struck the prostrate man with a board in such a way as to produce fracture of the back.

# 30 YEARS FOR MURDER.

## Czenovos Sentenced for Crime Over Fiddling Dispute.

[Special Dispatch to the Boston Herald.]

KEENE, N. H., Oct. 9, 1905. Vaschi Czenovos, 23 years. a woodchopper, of Fitzwilliam, who was indicted last week for the murder of Adam Carpisca at Fitzwilliam July 31. pleaded guilty today to murder in the second degree. and was sentenced to not less than 30 years or more than 32 years in state prison. The murder resulted from a fight over the question which was the better fiddler.

Clipping from the October
10, 1905 edition of *The
Boston Herald,* report-
ing on the sentencing of
Vaschi Czenovos.

In the absence of an autopsy, however, no definite evidence that the man's back was broken was produced at the hearing. The autopsy will be held tomorrow.

"Czenovos entered a plea of not guilty to the charge of murder, though he admitted the killing. He said that he struck Carpiska to get even with him but that he did not intend to kill him. Czenovos is about 20 years old."

Czenovos spent the next couple of months cooling his heels in jail, awaiting an indictment. Finally, on October 9, he was called before the New Hampshire supreme court, presided over by one Judge Peasler, to lodge a plea. It had been expected that he would plea not guilty; but for reasons that are unclear, he didn't make any plea at all. As he was taken back to jail, the press opined that the charge would be murder in the second degree, which carried with it a life sentence. At least, he would be spared the scaffold.

Czenovos' declining to make a plea didn't help him any; the next day, changed his mind and pled guilty, and

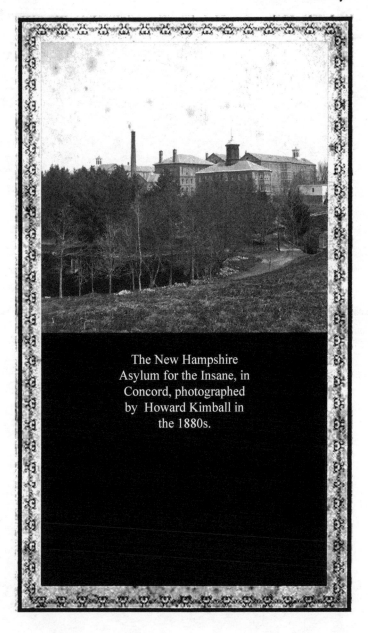

The New Hampshire
Asylum for the Insane, in
Concord, photographed
by Howard Kimball in
the 1880s.

was sentenced to 30 years in Concord State Prison.

We don't hear of Czenovos again until June of the following year. Apparently, in the interim, it was determined that he wasn't wrapped too tight, and was incarcerated in the New Hampshire Asylum for the Insane, situated in Concord.

It would appear that the security at this institution was somewhat lax, and Czenovos, with another inmate, made their escape on May 10. We have an account of this escapade, along with a somewhat blistering indictment of the authorities, in the June 4 edition of *The Boston Herald:*

### ESCAPED MADMEN ELUDE CAPTURE
*New Hampshire Fugitives Not Closely Followed by the Officials.*
*[Special Dispatch to the Boston Herald.]*

"CONCORD, N.H., June 2, 1907. Two of the most dangerous criminals ever convicted in New Hampshire escaped from the state insane asylum in this city May 10 and are still at large.

# ESCAPED MADMEN ELUDE CAPTURE

## New Hampshire Fugitives Not Closely Followed by the Officials.

[Special Dispatch to the Boston Herald.]

CONCORD, N. H., June 3, 1907. Two of the most dangerous criminals ever convicted in New Hampshire escaped from the state insane asylum in this city May 10 and are still at large.

Very little effort has been made to apprehend them; and even the police of Concord claim they never have received copies of the circulars announcing the disappearance of the men.

Headline from the June 4, 1907 edition of *The Boston Herald,* pertaining to the escape of Vaschi Czenovos and another inmate from the state lunatic asylum.

"Very little effort has been made to apprehend them; and even the police of Concord claim they never have received copies of the circulars announcing the disappearance of the men.

"One man, Vaschi Czenovos, is a murderer; the other, Frank R. Marsh, alias Lawrence Nelson Julian, is a burglar. Each, in his way, is as dangerous as Minot St. Clair Francis, whose marvelous escapes from the Massachusetts asylum at Bridgewater and the Maine state prison at Thomaston, are still themes of popular wonder, although the form of derangement is entirely dissimilar.

"Notwithstanding the dangerous character of the men and the serious nature of the offences for which they were serving time, no efforts to trace or locate them have been made beyond the sending of a few circulars to some of the larger cities of New England and the middle states and others to a score or so logging camps of Maine, New Hampshire and Vermont.

"None have been sent to the smaller

cities and towns, and the asylum authorities refused point blank to provide *The
Boston Herald* with photographs of the
couple, the representative seen stating
the superintendent had left orders that
nothing in regard to the matter should
be given to the newspapers, as the affair
was not one of interest to the public.

"Among police and prison officials
no little dissatisfaction is expressed
because of the apparent inactivity of the
asylum officials. It is freely declared that
the freedom of the two convicts is a constant menace, and the authorities assert
that either one is likely to commit overt
acts at any time.

"No rewards have been offered to
inspire the energy of police and county
officials throughout the eastern part
of the country, and no search has been
made in localities where the escaped
men might resort."

Given Czenovos' history, one might
be tempted to accuse these authorities of
criminal negligence. It would seem that
the staff at the New Hampshire Insane

Asylum weren't seeing anything particularly alarming at the fact that this character was now on the loose. This was a decision they would soon regret.

In early July, the body of Mrs. Annie H. Studley was discovered floating in Canobie Lake. There were quite a few aspects to the death that attracted the attention of the authorities. First off, it seems that she had been brained with a large stone, which was found at the site. Secondly, she apparently had a large quantity of opium in her stomach, probably due to the pills she had been taking. Then the family came forward, and informed the press that the woman had been incredibly depressed for since her estrangement from her husband, and they suspected suicide.

Right. So she bashed herself on the side of the head with a rock and then dove into the lake. Somehow, that doesn't sound very likely.

What makes this all the more interesting is that, immediately prior to the murder, Mrs. Studley had been observed

Graphic from the July 6, 1907
edition of *The Boston Journal*,
reporting on the murder at
Canobie Lake.

with a large quantity of cash upon her person. At one point, she peeled a five dollar bill off a huge wad that she had with her, in payment for her lodgings at the local hotel. When her body was discovered, however, it held only twenty-seven cents in change.

For a full account of the murder, we turn to the July 5, 1907 edition of *The Boston Journal:*

"Salem, N.H., July 4 — Developments today in the mystery surrounding the death of Mrs. Annie H. Studley of Boston, whose body was found floating in the waters of Canobie Lake Tuesday afternoon, not only strengthens the theory that the woman's death was a deliberate murder, but brought to light what may prove to be an important clue in the case.

## UNKNOWN, DEMENTED MAN RAN FROM SCENE

"An unknown man, said to have been demented, who had been hanging around Salem for two days before the crime was committed has been traced by reputable witnesses in the vicinity of the lake at or near the time of the crime, was seen by the man running away from the very spot which the woman's body was later found, and, more than that, was overheard by another, who told a *Journal* man, to remark that he had 'given her a slug' and that 'she is done for good and all.'

## BACKED BY WITNESSES

"These facts, backed as they are by the statements of witnesses, have made sufficient impression upon the sheriff to cause him to spread the description of the maniac broadcast and tomorrow he will seek the aid of every police department in New England to locate him and bring him back where he may be closely questioned. There is a possibility that the man may be able to explain his movement sufficiently to clear himself of the suspicion which now rests upon him but the evidence now in the hands of the authorities seems almost beyond any man's ability to disprove.

"The man whose description was given out to the newspapers by High

Sheriff Collis tonight was first seen on Saturday when he suddenly made his appearance in town, coming from nobody knows where. He hung about town Saturday and Sunday spending money freely and making friends with whoever chanced his way. Among those with whom he became acquainted was George Taylor, a hostler employed by Levi Wendbury at this estate, which borders Canobie Lake not far from Dow's Grove near where Mrs. Studey's body was later found.

## DROPS FROM SIGHT

"Mrs. Studley left Salem where she had been stopping since Friday shortly after 9 o'clock on Monday morning and it was about the same time that the demented man may suddenly dropped from view as quickly and mysteriously as he had appeared two days previously.

"Taylor the coachman has since told two Salem men, P. H. Knapp, a livery stable keeper and W. W. Harvey, who in turn reported the matter to the authorities, that some time Monday, as

# "I've done her for good and all !"

CRY OF MRS STUDLEY'S SUPPOSED SLAYER OVERHEARD DURING ROW IN A DERRY STREET.

# SLAIN BY MANIAC

## Detectives' Belief Now In Mrs. Studley Murder Case

Edward H. Watson,
Who heard demented man say I've done her for good"

### MAN SOUGHT IN STUDLEY MURDER

Height.................6 feet
Weight...........150 pounds
Complexion ............Dark
Eyes.............Large, hazel
Hair and mustache......Black
Build ................Slender
Clothes ..............Shabby
Demented.......Acts queerly

— — —

If you see him notify The Journal or the police.

### MAN SEEN FLEEING THROUGH WOODS FROM THE LAKE

George Taylor Heard Woman Scream and Describes Unknown Demented Man, Who Later, During Row With Companion in a Derry Street, Says "I've Done Her for Good!"

Headline from the July 5, 1907
edition of *The Boston Journal,*
reporting on the authorities' first
suspect in the Studley killing.

he was working about the Woodbury place he heard a woman's screams and a little later saw a man who he positively declares was the demented man, running through the woods from the direction of Dow's Grove. Knowing the man's condition, he did not think much of the affair at the time but after the finding of Mrs. Studley's body he connected the two and told of what he had seen and heard of the affair.

"As soon as High Sheriff Collis heard the story from Knapp and Harvey he decided to investigate and sent for Taylor to be brought before him. Unfortunately the man was out of town today and he had not returned at midnight but the sheriff is still waiting for him and as soon as he returns he will be interviewed on the subject and put through the third degree by the officials.

### SHERIFF BELIEVES STORY.

"Sheriff Collis however has perfect faith in the two men who reported the matter to him and is strongly impressed with their story. Both of the men then reiterated their stories to a *Journal* man.

"The next heard from the demented man was on Monday afternoon when he returned to Salem but this time stopped only a few minutes leaving town at 4 o'clock on a north-bound train. From that time until early Wednesday morning, when he was seen by a Derry man, Edward H. Watson, the man's movements are a mystery.

"It was 1:30 o'clock Wednesday morning when he was seen by Watson, according to the story which Watson told a *Journal* man and which was by him repeated to the sheriff. Watson was returning to his home, he says, when his attention was attracted by the sound of loud voices a short distance up the road, and as he drew near he saw two men, one whose description tallies exactly with that of the much sought maniac, and another, apparently a friend. The two men were talking in such loud voices that Watson, although some distance away, could distinctly her a large portion of their conversation.

## "GAVE HER A SLUG!"

"The unknown man, who Watson says was either very much excited or considerably under the influence of liquor, called his friend an uncomplimentary name. His comrade replied something which Watson did not catch and then remarked in a loud voice, 'I gave her a slug and she is done for good and all.' Who he referred to in his conversation or so much of it as reached Watson's ear is not explained but the supposition of suspicion naturally is that his remark had some connection with the Canobie Lake mystery.

"As Watson approached the two men they turned and walked hurriedly away from the Manchester road and disappeared. That is the last trace of the men thus far found, and the trail stops at present.

"High Sheriff Collis is hardly willing to be quoted as believing the demented man guilty of having committed murder but his actions and his anxiety to locate and question him indicate that he has suspicion He admits that the man's case demands investigation. Mr. Collis told a *Journal* man today that the Studley mystery was the most baffling that has ever come to his attention if not in the history of the State, and he and his deputies are working night and day in their efforts to unravel it.

"Sheriff Collis and Deputies Wesley Adams and Benjamin Wheeler paid another visit to Canobie Lake today to gather what additional evidence they might in the case and they found considerable amount of interest in connection with it.

## SAW WOMAN LEAVE TRAIN

"Their first efforts were to find someone who had actually seen Mrs. Studley after she left the train at the Canobie Lake station on Monday morning, and in this they were successful for they located a man who was hanging about the station when the morning train from Salem arrived and who directed a woman answering Mrs. Studley's description to the lake. They also found Joseph Lamson, the man who saw a woman's hat lying on a rock Monday morning and again when he passed with his wife on Monday afternoon and when showed Mrs. Studley's hat positively identified it as hers.

"There is only one point that is not yet entirely clear to the authorities, and that is how the body could have floated in the lake from Monday morning, the time set for the woman's death, until late Tuesday afternoon, when it was found by the Rev. Henry Chandler and dragged ashore by boats from the picnic groves about its shores as well as by the cottagers.

"Fred LeRock, a boatman for hire, says that he passed over the very spot where the body was later found shortly after 9 o'clock Monday morning which would be before the arrival of the woman at the park and after 11 o'clock he made half-hour trips over the same spot but at no time did he see any signs of a body or hear anything of a suspicious nature. Tuesday he landed a party at the same spot at 9:30 in the morning and again failed to see the body. This time he was accompanied by Charles Swazey and John Healey and they substantiated his statement.

## NO WATER IN LUNGS.

"The only explanation for this is that the woman's body had been sunk in a deeper section of the lake and had only just come to the surface when it was found. The medical referee still clings to his finding that there was no water on the lungs and that the woman did not drown, but was dead when she struck the water and the only way in which these two facts can be made to jibe is by a theory which is put forward that the body was weighted and after staying under the water until Tuesday had broken away from the weights and floated to shore.

"The only thing to substantiate this theory is the fact that when the body was found there was a small rope about the waist, to which her handbag was tied. The rope was what the officers describe as the largest size of bundle cord and while it is small they believe that it would have sufficient strength to hold a rock big enough and heavy enough to sink the body beneath the water.

"The action of the water and the constant tugging of the body, which because of the air in the lungs would have a strong tendency to seek the top of the water might have loosened the knots and allowed the rock or other weights to slip out. A point in favor of this way of figuring is the finding of the woman's handbag attached to this same rope as though an effort were being made to get every possible bit of evidence out of sight beneath the water.

"Taken all in all the theory of suicide which many of the officials and others sought to put forward from the first and to which they have vainly endeavored to cling is slowly but surely being broken up until there is hardly a point in its favor left at the present time to keep the theory alive.

"Deputy Sheriff Robert Scott was dispatched to Boston today to look up the past history of Mrs. Studley to see if he could find any connection between the woman and the much wanted demented man, but he has not yet reported back to Sheriff Collis."

Even as Mrs. Studley's brother, Fred Heyer of Boston, arrived in West Derry to claim his sister's body and take it back with him on the night train, the trail of the criminals was growing cold.

In their initial investigations, the police had arrested one John Neely of Nashua in connection with the killing. On July 8, Neely was transported from Peterborough to Concord, there to be confronted by George W. Taylor, the witness who had overheard the conversation between the alleged assailants at Canobie Lake. Upon seeing the suspect, however, Taylor emphatically declared that they had the wrong man, as the one he observed had been baldheaded, and Neely possessed a full head of hair.

This revelation sent the authorities into a tailspin. Another search was made of the murder site, this time under the gaze of a large crowd, drawn to the spot by morbid curiosity. The question of suicide again reared its ugly head, but there didn't seem to be much evidence to support it.

Meanwhile, the chief suspect, John Neely, was released and allowed to go on his way toward Wilton, a trip he was undertaking when arrested in Peterborough. An autopsy performed on July 9 determined that Mrs. Studley had died from a blow on the brain, and it was unlikely that this could have been self-inflicted. Mrs. Studley's relatives in Rockland, Maine, however, were still determined that the woman had killed herself, as she was distraught over her finances and declining health.

Finally, the search for the murderer began to focus on Vaschi Czenovos; unfortunately, nearly a week had passed since the killing, and he had gained plenty of time to make his escape. We have this account from the July 10, 1907 edition of *The Boston Herald:*

## HUNTING LUNATIC
## IN STUDLEY CASE

*Suspicion directed to Murderer Czenovos,*
*Fugitive from Asylum.*
*[Special Dispatch to the Boston Herald.]*

# HUNTING LUNATIC IN STUDLEY CASE

## Suspicion Directed to Murderer Czenovos, Fugitive from Asylum.

[Special Dispatch to the Boston Herald.]

DERRY. N. H., July 9, 1907. One of the suspects reported as being seen in the woods immediately after the body of Mrs. Annie H. Studley was found in Canobie lake, bears a striking resemblance to Vaschi Czenovos, one of the most dangerous criminals in New Hampshire, who recently escaped from the state insane asylum at Concord.

Headline from the July 10, 1907 edition of *The Boston Herald,* reporting on how authorities were now concentrating on Czenovos as the murderer in th Studley case.

"DERRY, N.H., July 9, 1907. One of the suspects reported as being seen in the woods immediately after the body of Mrs. Annie H. Studley was found in Canobie lake bears a striking resemblance to Vaschi Czenovos, one of the most dangerous criminals in New Hampshire, who recently escaped from the state insane asylum in Concord.

"Czenovos is a murderer and has been at large since May 10, since which time he has eluded every effort to capture him. Those who believe that Mrs. Studley was killed and her body thrown in the lake — and these are now numerous, since Medical Referee Newell has practically determined that the woman died from concussion of the brain — are beginning to connect Czenovos with the crime.

### HAD CONSIDERABLE MONEY.

"That Mrs. Studley had considerable money in her bag when she paid her hotel bill but a few hours before the dead body was found, and that she had but 27 cents when the bag was again searched, points to robberty as at least one of the reasons for the crime, if a crime was committed.

"That Czenovos had no money when he left the insane asylum; that he had to keep in hiding and hence could not obtain employment; that he was badly in need of money, are but possible reasons why he could have killed the woman.

"The attention of the county authorities has been called to the possibility of Czenovos being the man wanted and they have started a hunt for him. In this they will be aided in every way possible by the state asylum authorities.

### LOOKING FOR TAYLOR.

"From Salem it is learned that Sheriff Collis is in vain searching for George W. Taylor, the man who first reported seeing a demented man running through the woods on the afternoon when the body was found. On the description furnished by Taylor, John Neely, a Manchester man, was arrested, but Taylor failed to identify him as the man he had seen. Neely was released, and Taylor, who was but a voluntary witness, also dropped out of the case.

"Now the officials would like to interview Taylor again. Why, they will not say, for he has already been through the third degree and has been declared free of suspicion.

"Prof. Angell's report of the analysis of the stomach of the dead woman will be made to the medical referee tomorrow, and immediately the latter will forward his report on the autopsy to County Solicitor Batcheldor of Portsmouth."

After that, the trail runs cold. It seems that Sheriff Collis never did catch up with Czenovos, who simply disappeared. One would suspect that he took advantage of his head start, and lost himself in the lumberyards of northern Maine or Canada. And so ends this strange and brutal tale, engendered when one man determined that he was a better fiddle player than the other, and was willing to resort to murder to prove his proposition.

Ossaian E. Dodge, as a young man.

# FIVE
# THE SINGER AND THE THIEF

Sometimes, the strangest stories of this town originate with people who were just passing through. For instance, we have the tale of one Ossian Euclid Dodge, a mid-19th century minstrel who found himself in a highly peculiar position right here in town.

Dodge was born in Cayuga, N.Y., in 1820. By the age of five he showed himself to have significant musical leanings. Having made a vow of lifelong temperance to his mother, he determined to present the public with comic songs without the slightest hint of innuendo. "I will write my own songs," he said, "and the public shall learn that a comic song is not necessarily a vulgar one, and

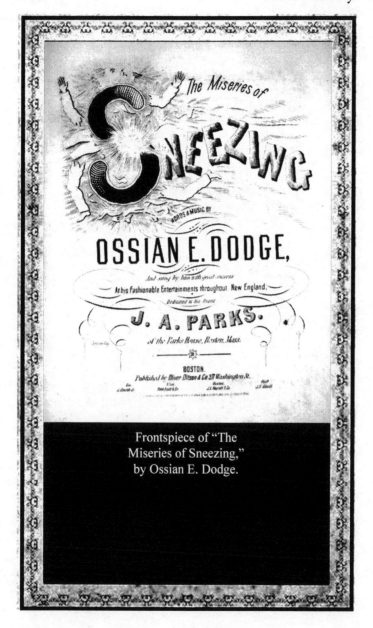

Frontspiece of "The Miseries of Sneezing," by Ossian E. Dodge.

that wit which has no fellowship with profanity or coarseness will be keenly relished by the best and most refined portions of society."

In the spring of 1846, Dodge was contracted to give a concert in Fitzwilliam, and it was at this time that he experienced an event that would profoundly affect the rest of his life. For a full account, we turn to the March 22, 1861 edition of the *Farmer's Cabinet:*

## THE EFFECT OF KINDNESS

"We learned on Saturday evening the particulars of a story which partakes of a romantic cast, but the truth of which can be vouched for. One of the principal actors in it is our well-known fellow-citizen and vocalist, Ossian E. Dodge.

"In the spring of the year 1846, Dodge was giving concerts in the New England States. Having to give a concert in Fitzwilliam, a town in New Hampshire, but a short distance from the Massachusetts line, he arrived at Winchendon, and he set out with a guitar bag in hand, with the purpose of walking the remaining five miles to Fitzwilliam, leaving his portmanteau to follow by stage the next day.

"About midway between the two places, in a lonely part of the road, a man sprang from a hiding place at the road-side, and grasped Dodge by the throat, demanding his money. Being as 'spry as a cat,' Dodge soon extricated himself from the grasp of the robber, flung him into the ditch, and wrested from him the cudgel with which he was armed. Instead of showing fight the man pleaded hard to be allowed to go in peace. As the manner of the man evidently showed that he was no habitual robber, Dodge promised to let him go on condition that he told him the reason for the attack. The man burst into tears, stating that nothing but starvation impelled him to the crime. He was a young man of respectable connection, but had been seduced by gay companions into habits of dissipation which had ended in leaving him without money or friends other than a young wife who clung to him in spite of everything. Finding no chance of getting a living in his native place, he had set out with his wife in hopes of obtaining a situation as a clerk in some other place, but although they visited a good many towns and villages, he had met with no success. To add to their misery and sufferings, the privations which they had endured, had hastened the period when the young wife was to become a mother, and she now lay in a barn at a short distance unable to proceed further, and in hourly expectation of giving birth to a child. With a wife in this position, with no money in his pockets and no food to eat, it was not astonishing that the wretched man had been driven to the desperate course of committing a highway robbery.

"Dodge heard the man's story, and at once requested him to show the way to the barn. Here the woman was found, and she confirmed every word of her husband's narrative. No time was to be lost, so, after assuring them that he would speedily return, Dodge set out at a rapid

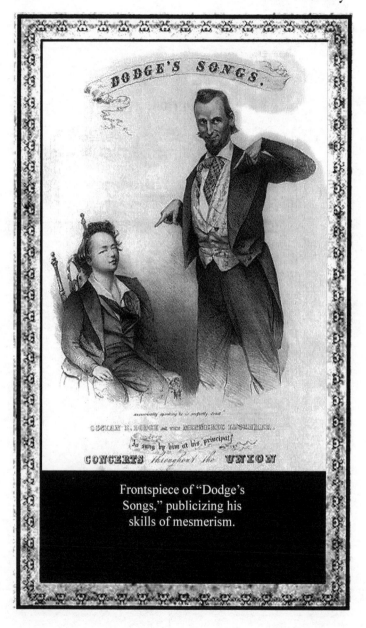

Frontspiece of "Dodge's Songs," publicizing his skills of mesmerism.

pace for Fitzwilliam. A horse and wagon were quickly obtained and driven out to the barn, when the unfortunate couple were taken to town and brought to the tavern. A doctor was procured, nourishing food supplied, and before morning a boy was born.

"Next evening the concert was given, and the entire proceeds, amounting to about forty-five dollars, were handed over to the now reformed and thankful husband. Before leaving the place Dodge interested many of the leading citizens in behalf of the couple, and left with the satisfaction of knowing that his proteges were no longer in danger of want.

"Nothing more had been heard of them by Mr. Dodge until Saturday evening last, when a well-dressed man entered his music store and enquired for him. Although the man gave his name, Dodge neither remembered name nor the person until reminded of the circumstances under which they met fourteen years ago. It seems that they had obtained a situation in Fitzwilliam, and

Frontspiece of "Ossian's Serenade."

remained there for nearly a year, when he joined a company of emigrants for the West. He had settled in Illinois, and had worked his way to comparative opulence and distinction, being at present a member of the Illinois legislature. His wife died about a year since, leaving no children except the boy who was born under such peculiar circumstances, and who has been named after the benefactor of the parents.

"The above particulars we learned from the gentleman himself. He is a remarkably frank, intelligent man, and is a favorable specimen of the Illinois legislator. At his request we have refrained from publishing his name whilst having free permission to use the details. What his history would have been had the night upon Dodge never occurred is a subject for conjecture, but it is highly probable that it would have been very different from what it has been."

There are a number of incidents of note in Dodge's later life, which, although having nothing to do with Fitzwilliam,

The so-called "Ultima Thule"
daggeurotype, picturing the famed
author Edgar Allan Poe.

are interesting in their own right. For instance, he was, for many years, the owner of a rare daguerreotype taken of the tragic and famous author Edgar Allan Poe, taken in 1846. The "Ultima Thule" daguerreotype, as it is commonly known, was stolen from the photographer Edwin Manchester in about 1860, and found itself in Dodge's possession shortly thereafter. He kept the image for the rest of his life, although its whereabouts are presently unknown.

In 1861, Dodge moved to St. Paul, Minnesota, along with his wife, Effie, and sons, Ossian, Jr. and Ethiel, to rooms on Fourth Street, between Washington and Franklin Street. According to record, their home life was anything but serene. Tiring of his wife's alleged abuse, Dodge sued for divorce in January of 1873.

"Ever since she was married, she has kept a six-barreled loaded revolver in her possession, with which she has a great many times threatened to blow my brains out and shoot me," he declared under oath. He further stated that his wife was in the habit of beating his son over the head "with a bathing-brush 20 inches long, and so severely as to break the handle of the brush." When this instrument was not available, he testified, she would then resort to using the tongs on the boy.

After this, things turned decidedly ugly. We have this account of the divorce proceedings from the August 15, 1874 edition of the *New York Herald*:

### OSSIAN'S DODGE.
**A Sequel to the St. Paul Scandal — After getting His Wife's Release of Dower and Selling All His Property, Dodge Waltzes Away Without Her.**

*[St. Paul Despatch to the **Chicago Times**.]*

"The readers of the *Times* during the months of January and February, 1873, will recollect the salient features in the Ossian E. Dodge scandal, with which our city was convulsed at that time. A case filled with more putrid nastiness, in which both parties appeared to be about equally guilty, it is hard to imagine. It will be remembered that the case was brought before the public gaze by Mrs. Dodge commencing proceedings for a divorce on the grounds of adultery, the main charge being based on the discovery of Ossian in bed in a sleeping room in his own house with a sewing girl of easy virtue. Dodge answered by filing numerous charges against his wife of having adulterous connection with various parties, on various occasions. For weeks the case was before the courts, the filthy details occupying columns of the city press. Finally, after both parties had proved their charges against each other, the case was settled, each condoning the other's conduct, and the affair ending in a resumption of marital relations. This action was so unnatural as to cause the greatest surprise. There were not a few, however, who knew Dodge well, and thought his intention was to get his property into his own hands, then desert his wife. This seems to be borne out by subsequent proceedings. Months ago Dodge announced that he should leave

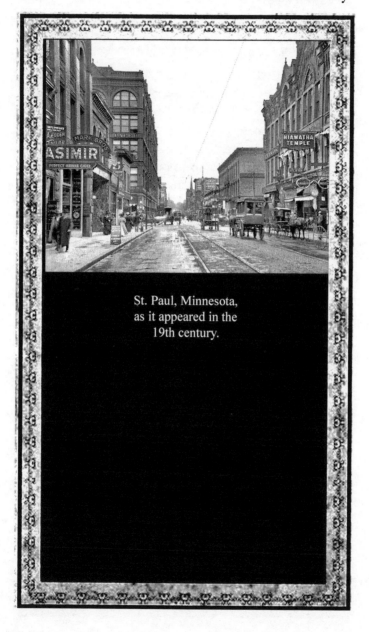

St. Paul, Minnesota,
as it appeared in the
19th century.

for the East as soon as he could dispose of his property. He has recently been selling his property, amounting in the aggregate to about $50,000, Mrs. Dodge signing the deeds jointly with her husband. This completed, Mrs. Dodge, the latter part of last week, went up to Rush City, forty-five miles distant, to visit friends. She was to return on Thursday evening and accompany her husband East. But Dodge, instead of waiting his wife's return, left with his two youngest children on Sunday evening, with the expressed determination of never seeing his wife again. It is reported that Mr. Dodge left a letter for his wife, that will be delivered to her on her arrival home; but its contents are as yet unknown. It is generally understood, however, that he made no settlement upon her, and left her with but a very small amount of ready funds; but that he has arranged for the payment to her of a regular stipend for her maintenance, so long as she conducts herself in a seemly manner. Much sympathy is manifested for Mrs.

Dodge, and a good deal of indignation that Ossian's sharp practice should have been so eminently successful."

Whatever respite Dodge got from the dissolution of his marriage was, however, somewhat short-lived. He died in November of 1876. His obituary, as published in the November 7 edition of the *London American Traveller* reads as follows:

### THE DEATH OF OSSIAN E. DODGE.

"We extremely regret that we have to announce the death of Mr. Ossian E. Dodge. Mr. Dodge, who is better known to our readers under the *nom de plume* of "Ivan Ort," it will be remembered, was a regular contributor for some time to the columns of the *Traveller* where many of his writings attracted the utmost attention and interest, especially his sketches of Palestine. Mr. Dodge, when he first entertained the idea of writing sketches of this nature, commenced a tour through Egypt, Assyria, and the Holy Land, and how well he carried out his idea and how thoroughly he performed his self-imposed task is superfluous for us to point out. Mr. Dodge was also well known in musical and dramatic circles, both in this country and the United States. He was for some time a correspondent for the *New York Sun,* and it may be of interest to know that this is the gentleman who created such a furore by purchasing a single-seat ticket for a concert, when Jenny Lind was in the zenith of her fame, for $500 in Boston. He was subsequently editor of the *Boston Weekly Museum.* Mr. Dodge was possessed of fine literary taste, and wielded a graceful pen as an essayist and correspondent. In literary and journalistic circles he made many friends, who admired him as much for his rare and attractive social qualities as for his extraordinary mental acquirements. He was 53 years old. For many years he was the Secretary of the Chamber of Commerce of St. Paul, Minn."

From this obituary, we can see that Dodge led an extraordinarily varied and interesting life, filled with equal portions

Frontspiece of "Ossian's Serenade," picturing Dodge being introduced to singer Jenny Lind by famed showman P.T. Barnum.

of accomplishment and scandal. But, perhaps, the high point of his career had to have come when, on a lonely road in Fitzwilliam, he aided a young family in dire need, and completely changed their lives.

*Photograph courtesy of John Fitzwilliam*
An engraved memorial to one Charles H.
Scott, a brakeman who was killed on the
Fitzwilliam railroad in 1870.

# SIX
# BLOOD ON
# THE TRACKS

Recently, my good friend John Fitz-william alerted me to a particular artifact that he thought may be of interest in the context of this book. It seems that, in the late Victorian period, there was something of a fad for little memorial souvenirs — an engraved metal frame with a photograph of the deceased, along with the name and circumstances of the demise of the individual in question.

Well, this one was dedicated to one Charles H. Scott, who, according to the inscription, was "Acidentaly *[sic]* killed at Fitzwilliam, N.H., Aug. 25, 1870. Aged 26 years."

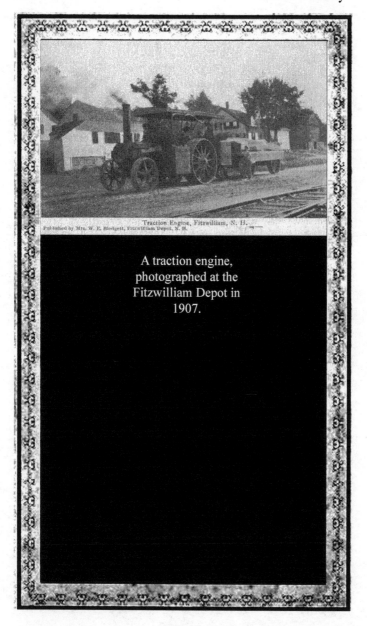

Traction Engine, Fitzwilliam, N. H.
Published by Mrs. W. E. Blodgett, Fitzwilliam Depot, N. H.

A traction engine,
photographed at the
Fitzwilliam Depot in
1907.

I did some research on this poor fellow, and discovered that he was a resident of Fitchburg, Massachusetts. Apparently, on this one afternoon, he managed to get himself squashed between a couple of freight cars at the Fitzwilliam Depot, and died instantly.

Although the railroad brought prosperity to the little town by supporting the nascent granite mining industry, there were still conflicts between the iron horses and the flesh and blood variety favored by the agrarian locals.

Beginning in 1845, there was a concerted effort to bring the Cheshire Railroad into southern New Hampshire, two routes being seriously considered for the new venture, one of which would pass through Richmond, the other through Fitzwilliam.

A public hearing was held at the Fitzwilliam Meeting House. At this point, one Daniel Spaulding, a prominent local citizen, expressed his desire that the route go through Fitzwilliam, and promised $5,000 to back it up.

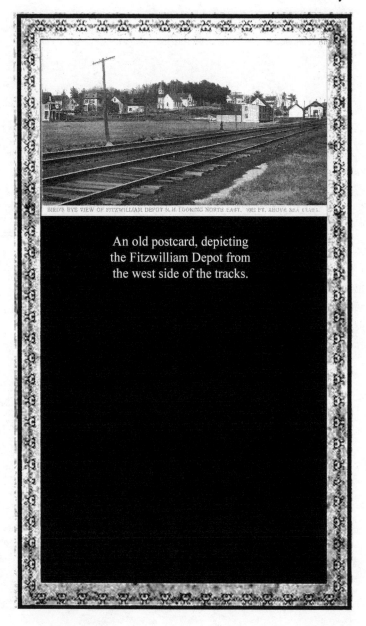

BIRD'S EYE VIEW OF FITZWILLIAM DEPOT N.H. LOOKING NORTH EAST,  1065 FT. ABOVE SEA LEVEL.

An old postcard, depicting
the Fitzwilliam Depot from
the west side of the tracks.

There was a considerable amount of resistance to this proposal; it was determined by many that the hilly terrain would create a considerable problem in creating a viable track. Spaulding suggested that the promoters should stay overnight in town, and he would review the site with them in the morning, showing how this expense could be obviated. This plan was readily assented, and the survey made. This time, the promoters were convinced, and work began on the new track.

Irish laborers were brought in to work on the railroad for the next three years, and the route was finally opened on May of 1848. It would be no exaggeration to say that this event profoundly changed the character of the town; thousands of passengers moved through Fitzwilliam every year, and 2,000 tons of freight entered the town annually, another 10,000 tons leaving, primarily as a result of the burgeoning granite industry. One George W. Parker was the Fitzwilliam station agent, and the first President was

Thomas E. Edwards. Lucien Tilton was the first Chief Engineer, being responsible for much of the layout of the original track. The elevation of the railroad was 1151 feet at its highest point, the length being about nine miles.

Almost immediately, the new route had its problems. As recounted by Worcester, Massachusetts resident W. J. Fletcher back in June, 1958, the engine "Monadnock" exploded at Bull Run near Fitzwilliam right at the opening of the track, killing the engineer and injuring the fireman. In 1857, a boiler explosion on the "Monadnock" blew out the front and the rear ends of the engine, instantly killing engineer Edward Corning and severely burning fireman Edward Whelm.

There was much more. We have this report from the March 9, 1848 edition of the *Keene Sentinel:*

"We hear that the evening train on the Cheshire Railroad ran over and killed an Irishman about dusk on Tuesday, three or four miles below Fitzwilliam, cutting off both his legs below the knee and one arm. He was lying upon the track and was doubtless intoxicated, as the engineer gave ample warning by bell and whistle when he discovered him, though too late to stop the train. As soon as possible the train ran back to the place of the accident, but he evidently lived but a few moments."

A little over a decade later, we have this sad tale of the demise of a family, as reported in the February 6, 1861 edition of the *Massachusetts Spy:*

"SAD FATALITY — In a brief paragraph we announced, yesterday, the death of a woman and child while crossing the railroad track in Fitzwilliam, N.H., on Friday last. We have since learned that the victims were the wife and child of Mr. Alonzo Damon of Hubbardston, with whom they were riding home from Fitzwilliam. Their horse, becoming frightened, rushed wildly upon the railroad track, when the engine overtook them, dashing the sleigh to pieces and killing the horse. Mr. Damon was thrown over the track and escaped serious injury, but

### Brakeman Killed.

Harvey T. Fields of Bellows Falls, a brakeman on the Cheshire road, fell from his train near Fitzwilliam summit, Monday night, and was run over and instantly killed. Both legs were cut off, the head injured and the body otherwise mutilated. Fields was the head brakeman on No. 17 freight, Charles Taggart conductor. He rode up the grade on the engine, as it is customary for the forward brakeman to do in cold weather, and when the train got nearly to the top of the hill, he went out upon the train to attend to the brakes. The last that was seen of him was the light of his lantern as he passed back upon the train. Noticing that the train gained speed as it began to run down hill toward Fitzwilliam, the fireman went out to help set the brakes, and it was soon

Notice in the December 25, 1889 edition of the *New Hampshire Sentinel,* pertraining to the death of brakeman Harvey T. Fields, who was killed near the Fitzwilliam summit.

his wife and child were instantly killed. Their bodies were horribly mutilated, that of the little child being picked up in nine pieces. The sad accident has thrown a gloom over Hubbardston, as Mrs. Damon was a woman greatly beloved in the community."

There was another tragic accident on the line in the Christmas season of 1889, involving a brakeman by the name of Harvey T. Fields. Here is the report as it came from the December 25 edition of the *New Hampshire Sentinel:*

### BRAKEMAN KILLED

"Harvey T. Fields of Bellows Falls, a brakeman on the Cheshire Road, fell from his train near Fitzwilliam summit, Monday night, and was run over and instantly killed. Both legs were cut off, the head injured and the body otherwise mutilated. Fields was the head brakeman on No. 17 freight, Charles Taggart conductor. He rode up the grade on the engine, as it is customary for the forward brakeman to do in cold weather, and when the train got nearly to the top

# FREIGHTS WRECKED.

## HEAD COLLISION OF TWO HEAVY TRAINS NEAR TROY.

**Engineers and Firemen Jump for Their Lives—One Brakeman Slightly Injured—Two Locomotives and Ten Cars Smashed to Pieces—The Blockade Cleared Away Tuesday Morning.**

A bad freight train wreck occurred on the Cheshire division of the Fitchburg road between six and seven o'clock Monday evening. The wreck took place near "Farrar's Crossing," just beyond the old pottery, on the road from Marlboro' depot to Troy. The collision was doubtless the most violent that ever occurred on the Cheshire road, and although there was no loss of life excepting the premature killing of a dozen or two of fat hogs, the destruction of property must have been large. Old railroad men who have been on the Cheshire division for years, say they never saw a collision which showed such evidences of the terrible force with

Report from the July 8, 1891 edition of *Thw New Hampshire Sentinel,* pertaining to a head-on collision between two trains.

of the hill, he went out upon the trains to attend to the brakes. The last that was seen of him was the light of his lantern as he passed back upon the train. Noticing that the train gained speed as it began to run down hill toward Fitzwilliam, the fireman went out to help set the brakes, and it was soon seen that Fields was not aboard. The train was stopped at Fitzwillam and the engine and train men returned, soon finding the remains of their comrade.

"Fields had worked for the Cheshire road several years as one of the car inspectors at Bellows Falls, and recently began braking. He was thirty years old and leaves a wife, but no children. The remains were taken charge of at Fitzwilliam by Undertaker Shedd, who went down on the No. 1 train and were taken to Bellows Falls or North Walpole, Tuesday morning. Deceased held a Travelers accident policy for $100."

In 1891, a head-on collision of two trains just outside of town resulted in the premature slaughter of a number of hogs, although the engineers were able to leap to safety. We have a report from the July 8 edition of the *New Hampshire Sentinel*, which extols the details of this cataclysmic crash:

## FREIGHTS WRECKED HEAD COLLISION OF TWO HEAVY TRAINS NEAR TROY.

*Engineers and Firemen Jump for Their Lives — One Brakeman Slightly Injured — Two Locomotives and Ten Cars Smashed to Pieces — The Blockade Cleared Away Tuesday Morning.*

"A bad freight train wreck occurred on the Cheshire division of the Fitchburg road between six and seven o'clock Monday evening. The wreck took place near 'Farrar's Crossing,' just beyond the old pottery, on the road from the Marlboro' depot to Troy. The collision was doubtless he most violent that ever occurred on the Cheshire road, and although there was no loss of life excepting the premature killing of a dozen or two of fat hogs, the destruction of property must have been large. Old railroad men who have been on the Cheshire division of years, say they never saw a collision which showed such evidences of the terrible force with which the two trains met, and in which so many cars were ground up before the momentum of the on-coming trains was subdued. The lucky escape of employees from serious injury is a source of surprise as well as congratulation to all.

"What the true cause of the accident was is not officially announced by the officers on the road, but the story of all the train men who were at the wreck seems to agree, and leaves no apparent doubt as to what took place. The trains which collided were Nos. 14 and extra 13. No. 14 consisted of about twenty-four cars, drawn by engine 237, one of the new Cheshire moguls, the train being in charge of Engineer T.A. Bartlett of this city and Conductor Geo. W. Toblas of Bellows Falls. This train was moving North. Extra No. 13 was a heavy hog train of over twenty cars, going South, and in charge of Conductor Dexter

Burbee and Engineer Michael Hickey, of Keene, and was drawn by engine No. 233. Extra 13 was following train No. 13 on red signals, thus having the same time table rights as the first No. 13. Train 14 met the first section of train 13, at Fitzwilliam, according to orders, but none of the men on No. 14 saw the red signals carried by this train for the second section. They thus supposed the track was clear for them to proceed to Keene. Extra 13 had the right of road to Troy to meet No. 14, and was proceeding accordingly. This train thus had the right to be where it was, but No. 14 should have awaited the arrival at Troy. The failure of the men on train 14 to observe the red signals carried by No. 13, caused the accident.

"At the point where the collision occurred there are curves in the road. The train from Troy came along through a gravel cut within a few rods of the point of collision, but how much of a curve there is in the track above this cut, we do not know. The engineer of the train going East could not have seen the West-bound train until it was nearly upon him. Persons who live nearby say that the two engineers whistled for brakes nearly at the same time. Engineer Hickey applied the air brake with which his train was equipped. This gave warning to the rear brakeman and Conductor Burbee, who were in the saloon car, and to the engine which was pushing. The brakes had brought this train nearly to a standstill when the collision occurred. Engineer Bartlett whistled for brakes and reversed his engine. This train was not equipped with air brakes. The engineers and firemen of both trains then jumped for their lives — and it was fortunate they did so. Conductor Tobias jumped from the top of his train and some of the brakemen on each train jumped also. Brakeman Fred Bello, of Keene, was setting up a brake when the engines met. He was thrown from the cars and received a sprained ankle, a dislocated shoulder and other bruises. He was attended by Dr. Stone, who put his shoulder in place and made him comfortable, and was then brought to Keene on the first train.

"Those who were eye witnesses of the collision say it was a most imposing sight. The two huge mogul engines met with a terrific shock, and plunged into each other as far as iron and iron could be driven together. They seemed to jump up and then settle back again into a solid mass, having been welded together by the shock. But still the cars in rear kept coming on.. The tenders were thrown up high into the air, and car after car of train 14 was driven against the engine and crushed into splinters by those in rear. Some six cars of this train were telescoped into a huge pile of debris and wreckage piled in rear of the locomotive and on either side. One car struck the bank twenty feet from the track and ten feet above it, leaving a big hole in the dirt and afterwards rolling down near the rails again. The tank of engine 237 was thrown across the roadway, to the left, and lay upon its side. The cab roof from the engine was over beyond the tank.

In rear of the boiler where the cab and tender should be, was a mass of broken tracks and timbers piled one above the other, several feet higher than the boiler. Had anyone remained on the engine they would have been ground to atoms. In rear of this pile were sections of cars laying in every direction, but not so finely pulverized as those closer to the engines.

"The tender of engine 233 stood upon its forward end, with car and tender trucks piled under it. The forward end of the first car of this train was forced up, but the air brakes were set and the cars did not telescope, although the buffers were all jammed close together for several cars back. Here the train broke to one side,. One car was tipped over upon the bank and the top was torn off another. The rest of the train remained on the track. A lot of hogs from the broken cars got out, several were killed and the remainder were liberated as soon as the wrecking train force could do so. John Lahill, who lives nearby, carried the news to Troy, and the steamer

# THREE KILLED IN CROSSING CRASH

## Two Women and Man in Car Struck by the Montreal Express

## STATE LINE, N. H., SCENE OF TRAGEDY

**[Special Dispatch to The Herald]**

WINCHENDON, Oct. 24—Two women and a man were killed near here tonight by the Montreal Express of the B. & M. railroad which left here at 10 p. m. The crash occurred at State Line, N. H., at the depot crossing, when the flier hit a closed motor car, utterly smashing it and hurling parts of it through the station windows into the waiting room

Report on the fatal crossing crash at State Line, as reported in the October 25th 1925, edition of *The Boston Herald*.

was soon on the ground. It is surprising the wreck did not take fire from engine 237 but the steamer was not needed.

"The wrecking gang arrived from Keene about 9:30, and during the night a wreck train from Fitchburg came up. Work was thus pushed from both ends of the wreck, after daylight. The broken cars were disposed of pretty fast after the men got fairly to work. The running parts of the engines, except the trucks, were not much broken, and the machines stood straight in line with the track and were placed on the iron again with comparative ease. About ten this morning the tracks were cleared and trains began to pass again. The wreckers made a remarkably quick job of it. Master Mechanic Leach, Foreman Follansbee and the wreck man from Fitchburg superintended their work."

As spectacular as this wreck undoubtedly was, it appears that virtually all of the men involved in the crash escaped with their skin intact, the only real casualties being that of a number of hogs.

The Webb Quarry, as seen
from the Fitzwilliam Depot,
from a 19th-century postcard.

A much more serious tragedy occurred at the State Line Station, on the border between Fitzwilliam and Winchendon, back in 1925. You can see the site of the area by driving down Route 12, and stopping as you reach the Winchendon line. The remains of the old train tracks are still visible, stretching out along the wetlands toward the center of town. There's a liquor and tobacco store there now, taking advantage of New Hampshire's comparatively liberal regulations concerning those products.

For a full account of the crash, we turn to the October 25 edition of *The Boston Herald:*

### THREE KILLED IN
### CROSSING CRASH
### TWO WOMEN AND MAN
### IN CAR STRUCK BY
### MONTREAL EXPRESS
### STATE LINE, N.H.,
### SCENE OF TRAGEDY

*[Special Dispatch to the Herald]*
"WINCHENDON, Oct. 24 — Two women and a man were killed near

here tonight by the Montreal Express of the B. & M. railroad which left here at 10 p.m. the crash occurred at State Line, N.H., at the depot crossing, when the flier hit a closed motor car, utterly smashing it and hurling parts of it through the station windows into the waiting room.

"A slight fire was started by gasoline on the outside of the building but was quickly put out. The dead are:

"MRS. GERTRUDE F. LAHIFF, a widow, of Leominster.

"MISS ROSE O'NEIL, of Keene, N.H.

'JAMES A. O'KEEFE, 168 Main Street, Leominster, a taxi driver.

"Identification of the women was not made until a very late hour, and was finally possible only when two men from Leominster, acquaintances of the women, came here to look at the bodies after hearing of the accident.

### JUST OVER THE STATE LINE

"The scene of the accident is about three and one-half miles from here and just over the state line in New Hampshire. The police of this town were early on the scene, headed by Chief Robert Callahan, with authorities from Leominster, and Fitzwilliam, N.H., in which township the accident occurred. At that time the only victim identified as O'Keefe, and this only through the finding of the registration for his car in his clothing.

"It is thought that the car was hired by the women from O'Keefe to drive them to Miss O'Neill's home in Keene, and that they were on their way north from here.

"There was no one on the scene at the time, but the crash brought several within a few minutes. The remains of the motor car, which was literally torn to pieces, were on this side of the railroad tracks. Part of it had been thrown against the depot building, smashing the windows.

"After the arrival of the medical referee from Keene, N.H., he ordered the authorities of Fitzwilliam to have

*Photograph by the author*
The Fitzwilliam railroad,
facing west, as it looks today.

the bodies sent here to the undertaking room of Charles E. Snow, and it was here that identification was finally made by the friend of the women who came from Leominster. After viewing the bodies they went to police headquarters where they made a report of what information they could give to Chief Callahan."

With the decline of the quarries, and subsequently of the railroad itself, the incidence of train-related accidents obviously disappeared. Unfortunately, this also meant the beginning of numerous car accidents. Well, I won't go into that here. Suffice it to say, even though technology continues to progress, there will always be tragedies.

## MURDER.

*Boston, May* 8.—We are informed, that there are now in custody six persons charged with murder, lately taken up in Fitzwilliam, in New-Hampshire. The circumstances, as nearly as we can recollect them, are as follows :—

A farmer in Vermont, about nine years ago, owing to some discontent, on the part of his wife, sold his farm, with the intention of settling in some part of New-Hampshire. He came to Swansey, about 12 or 14 miles from Fitzwilliam, for the purpose of examining the farms, in that vicinity.— Thinking he might have a better opportunity to examine those which were for sale, by travelling on foot, especially as the snow

An account of an 1810 murder in Fitzwilliam, as recounted in the June 3, 1819 edition of the *Bangor (Maine) Weekly Register.*

# SEVEN
# RANDOM
# VIOLENCE

As with many small towns, isolated violent incidents have occurred within this village over the years. In this chapter, I have endeavored to chronicle odd cases of mayhem which really don't have the legs to justify a longer narrative of their own.

To start with, we have an account of a man who came to Fitzwilliam in about 1810, with the purpose of purchasing a farm in Fitzwilliam. For those who are familiar with my book, *Mysteries of Monadnock*, they will find certain similarities between this case and the 1804 situation of Levi Haskell, who allegedly murdered one Seth Lucas, who had come into the area with the objective of buying a farm in Woodstock. He began drinking with Lucas and his associate, at which point Haskell offered to sell him his own spread down on Quarry Road. If he wished, he said, Lucas could come and check it out for himself.

He followed Haskell and his friend out into the road, and was never seen alive again.

For the next 14 years, Haskell's barn had been the object of local gossip, as residents reported hearing strange screams and seeing weird lights within. When the whole situation came to light some 14 years later as the barn burned to the ground, and human remains were found within. Haskell was indicted for murder, but was let off, as the case had gone completely cold.

Getting back to the subject, let us look into the 1810 murder. The following account comes from the June 3, 1819 edition of the *Bangor (Maine) Weekly Register:*

### MURDER.

"Boston, May 8. — We are informed,

that there are now six persons charged
with murder, lately taken up in Fitzwilliam, in New-Hampshire. The circumstances, as nearly as we can recollect
them, are as follows: —

"A farmer in Vermont, about nine
years ago, owing to some discontent, on
the part of his wife, sold his farm, with
the intention of settling in some part of
New-Hampshire. He came to Swanzey,
about 12 or 14 miles from Fitzwilliam,
for the purpose of examining the farms,
in that vicinity. — Thinking he might
have a better opportunity to examine
those which were for sale, by traveling
on foot, especially as the snow was then
deep; he left his horse at Swanzey, in the
care of a friend, and went with a considerable sum of money, to Fitzwilliam.

"Here he entered a store, and made
known that his object was to buy a farm,
for which he would pay cash, at the time
of purchase. Among a number of persons
present, two invited him to walk out with
them, and view some in that neighborhood. It being a moon-light evening, he

consented. He went; but never returned. It was, of course, supposed, that he was murdered by those who took him out, or by their accomplices.

"Another circumstance strengthened this supposition. Two men had been hunting foxes, on the day of the stranger's arrival; and having driven one into his burrow about dark, they stopped the entrance, and came very early the next morning, to dig him out. They found the ground had been newly thrown up; and supposed some person or persons had been there searching for the fox. They, however, proceeded to dig for him; and were astonished to find a hole sufficiently large to admit a man's body. They caught the fox, and concluded to keep what they had seen a secret; but on their way home, near a rivulet, they found an entire suit of clothes. They then related what they had seen to their neighbors; and we understand, curiosity was somewhat excited, and considerable search and inquiry made, but without effect.

"A year ago last winter, a barn was

burnt in Fitzwilliam, with most of its contents. On clearing away the rubbish, after the fire had subsided, it was found that part of the floor, on which a large quantity of hay had been placed, was not consumed. On removing this, a human skeleton presented itself to the astonished spectators.

"This was at once conjectured to be the remains of the before mentioned stranger. A number of suspicious persons were then taken up; but as nothing could be proved against them, they were discharged. Lately, clearer evidence having been produced, the six persons above mention, have been taken into custody; and a man, who was supposed to be one of the murderers, has disappeared, and not since been heard of."

• • •

We also have another account of a vicious assault, perpetrated on one Thomas Starkey, a resident of Troy, who was attacked in Fitzwilliam, while taking a load of furniture to Winchendon, Massachusetts, along present-day

## MURDEROUS ASSAULT.

**Thomas Starkey of Troy Assailed by Tramps—He is Struck on the Head with a Wagon Stake and Left in a Precarious Condition—The Assailants Arrested and Locked in Jail.**

Thomas Starkey of Troy was severely beaten by two tramps in Fitzwilliam Thursday afternoon, and now lies in a precarious condition. Mr. Starkey is a teamster and Thursday morning he left Troy with a load of furniture which he took to Winchendon, his boy following close behind with another load.

After delivering the furniture Mr. Starkey started home and when he reached State Line two tramps boarded his team ostensibly for a ride. When Fitzwilliam was reached one of the tramps took hold of Mr. Starkey and commenced squabbling with him, while the other picked up a wagon stake and struck him a heavy blow upon the head. The tramps then jumped from the team and a Mr. Baker, who lives near the place where the assault was committed, went to Mr. Starkey's assistance.

A vicious assault in Fitzwilliam, as reported in the September 2, 1891 edition of the *New Hampshire Daily Sentinel.*

Route 12. The whole unfortunate affair was imparted in an article published in the September 2, 1891 edition of the *New Hampshire Sentinel:*

## MURDEROUS ASSAULT.

**Thomas Starkey of Troy Assailed by Tramps — He is Struck on the Head with a Wagon Stake and Left in a Precarious Condition — The Assailants Arrested and Locked in Jail.**

"Thomas Starkey of Troy was severely beaten by two tramps in Fitzwilliam Thursday afternoon, and now lies in a precarious condition. Mr. Starkey is a teamster and Thursday morning he left Troy with a load of furniture which he took to Winchendon, his boy following close behind with another load.

"After delivering the furniture Mr. Starkey started home and when he reached State Line two tramps boarded his team ostensibly for a ride. When Fitzwilliam was reached one of the tramps took hold of Mr. Starkey and commenced squabbling with him, while the other picked up a wagon stake and struck him a heavy blow upon the head. The tramps then jumped from the team and a Mr. Baker, who lives near the place where the assault was committed, went to Mr. Starkey's assistance.

"The wounded man was removed to Mr. Baker's house, and Officer Wheelock notified. The officer harnessed his horse and with two or three others, started in pursuit of the tramps, who were overtaken about half a mile from the place where the assault was committed. When first seen they were just leaving the highway and entering the woods.

"The officer and his assistants left the team as soon as they reached the place where the men were seen to leave the highway and separating from each other formed a line to commence a search. By this time — seven o'clock — it was quite dark in the woods and it was through the strategy of Officer Wheelock that the assailants were captured as quickly as they were. As soon as the struck into the woods he shouted to his men, 'Draw your revolvers on them,' and then feigning to see the tramps shouted, 'Halt! You are under arrest. Throw up your hands.' He then called out again to his men, 'Shoot them if they move.' The next minute they came upon the prisoners, both of whom were standing together, with their hands held up, as commanded by the officer. Neither Officer Wheelock nor his assistants had seen the men, nor did they know they were near them; but succeeded in outwitting them by Mr. Wheelock's plan.

"The prisoners were at once handcuffed and taken to the town hall in Fitzwilliam where they were kept until the arrival of the night express. They were then brought to this city and placed in the lock-up.

"Dr. Hubbard was called to the wounded man and found a large gash cut in his head which was sewed up. Mr. Starkey remained unconscious throughout the night — or in a semi-conscious state — and suffered several slight hemorrhages.

### PRISONERS ARRAIGNED.

"The prisoners were arraigned before

Justice Holmes Friday morning and gave their names as Thomas Brown and Edward J. Corbett. These are not believed to be their true names as one of the Fitchburg train men identified one of them as Edward Durgin. The men both claimed to have no place of residence or occupation other than that of laborers. When accused of being tramps one of them protested against the name, claiming they always had money and never asked anyone for anything but work.

"From the testimony of the witnesses in court, it was difficult to determine whether the assault was made with the intention of robbery or only because of drunkenness. Both prisoners were drunk at the time and both claim they knew nothing of the assault until told of it this morning.

"Mr. Barker, who witnessed the affair from a distance, says that when the blow was struck with the cart stake, the stake struck the side of the wagon and thus diverted the blow from Mr. Starkey's head. Otherwise, he would almost certainly have been killed.

"Mr. Starkey's condition was such, Friday that his physician would not allow him to be brought to Keene to appear at the court, although was able to be removed to his home in Troy during the day.

"Mr. Starkey's boy, who is only about twelve years old, and was driving the team directly behind his father's, was the first one to notify Officer Wheelock of the assault and when the team started out to capture the men he was one of the occupants of the wagon.

"While the men were confined in the town hall at Fitzwilliam, awaiting their removal to this city, they were kept under close surveillance, as they watched every possible chance of escape.

"Justice Holmes decided that the case was of too grave a nature to come under his jurisdiction for trial, and bound the prisoners over in bonds of $1,000 each for their appearance at the October term of the court. Being unable to procure bonds they were taken to the jail to await trial."

• • •

When we think of Prohibition, and the inevitable liquor-running that went with it, our thoughts generally turn to those famous big-city gangsters from Chicago and New York, such as Al Capone and "Legs" Diamond. The idea that they would be running through the quiet little town of Fitzwilliam seems absurd.

On August 13, 1924, however, the Town Common became the scene of a violent confrontation between federal and state officers and a notorious liquor runner from Leominster, Mass., by the name of Joseph Visalli. He and an associate, one William Devoid of Keene, had hoped to evade the authorities by taking back roads. On this day, however, luck was not with them.

It seems that the authorities had set up a "liquor trap" — basically, a roadblock — in the center of town with the express purpose of halting and appending any individual who might be transporting alcohol through the area.

For the full details of this little imbroglio, we turn to the August 14 edition of *The Boston Herald:*

### CAUGHT IN LIQUOR TRAP, MAN ESCAPES
#### Pursued and Captured; Car Injures One

*[Special Dispatch to The Herald]*

"KEENE, N.H., Aug. 13 — Ordered to stop by federal and state officers who had laid a liquor trap below Fitzwilliam Centre, last night, Joseph Visalli of Leominster, Mass., made a pretense of getting out of the car and then shot his automobile ahead, throwing an officer off the car. He proceeded at a high rate of speed through the centre village, knocking down Frederick A. Tisdale of Dorchester, Mass. Tisdale was taken to the Fitzwilliam Tavern, suffering from a double fracture of the left ankle.

"Pursuing officers caught Visalli in Troy and took him to Fitzwilliam, where he was turned over to Deputy Sheriff Tucker. Several shots fired after

# CAUGHT IN LIQUOR TRAP, MAN ESCAPES

## Pursued and Captured; Car Injures One

[Special Dispatch to The Herald]

KEENE, N. H., Aug. 13—Ordered to stop by federal and state officers who had laid a liquor trap below Fitzwilliam Centre, last night, Joseph Visalli of Leominster, Mass., made a pretense of getting out of the car and then shot his automobile ahead, throwing an officer off the car. He continued at a high rate of speed through the centre village, knocking down Frederick A. Tisdale of Dorchester, Mass. Tisdale was taken to the Fitzwilliam Tavern, suffering from a double fracture of the left ankle.

A report from the August 14, 1924 edition of *The Boston Herald*, describing the attempted apprehension of liquor runners in Fitzwilliam.

the escape failed to halt the car. Bullets pierced the rear of the machine.

"Three charges were brought against Visalli: Refusing to stop after an accident, illegal transportation of liquor and illegal transportation. Bail was set at $500 on each of the liquor charges and at $800 on the charge of refusing to stop after the accident. He was held in $1500 bonds. The case will be heard in municipal court, Friday. Visalli's car was seized by the federal officer.

"William Devoid of Keene, caught in the same trap, was in court today on two charges, illegal possession of liquor and illegal transportation. Through his counsel he entered a plea of not guilty."

• • •

On a hot summer day back in August of 1966, a 13-year-old girl walked into the General Store adjacent to the depot, intending to buy some basic groceries. Nothing strange about that; it happens every day. What the man at the register didn't know, however, was that she was being watched by her abductor, a former

Steven H. Caouette,
pictured with his 13-year-
old love interest, Marie
Couture, in happier days.

mental patient. Even now, he was hiding in the grass outside, covering the building with a rifle.

The whole drama had started the previous Thursday, when one Steven H. Caouette broke into the home of the Couture family in Winchendon, Massachusetts, with the intention of abducting their daughter, Marie. Apparently, the two had been dating for some time, and she decided to initiate a break-up.

Evidently, he didn't take it well.

The whole drama was played out in various Boston newspapers, including the *Boston Herald* and the *Boston Traveler*. We have here the story as it originally broke on August 19, according to United Press International:

## POLICE HUNT GIRL, YOUTH IN ABDUCTION

"WINCHENDON, Mass. (UPI) — Police officers with bloodhounds searched a densely wooded area Thursday night for a 13-year-old girl reported abducted from her home by an armed ex-Marine.

"Officer George Higgins said Marie Couture was reported missing by her aunt about 4 p.m. after Steven Caouette, 19, forced the girl from the house. Police said Caouette, a former mental patient, was armed with a knife and a loaded .21 rifle.

"'It's loaded, absolutely the rifle is loaded. We don't know what might happen.'

"Higgins said at least six state troopers from area barracks rushed to the scene. Spotlights and bloodhounds were being used in the search.

"The area is dense woods with no roads, but Boston and Albany Railroad tracks lead into the area."

More details on the couple's escape can be found in this piece from the *Boston Traveler*, published the same day:

"In the home at the time was the girl's aunt, Shirley Morancie, 29.

"She said Caouette warned her, 'If you say anything about this, I'll shoot you.

"Two young boys living in the area told police they saw Caouette 'pushing and pulling the girl out of the house and down the street.'

"They said he pointed his rifle at them and threatened to shoot them if they called police.

"Since the couple vanished several persons have reported seeing them in various parts of this border town.

"Bloodhounds traced the girl's scent yesterday to the shore of Whitney Pond and there lost it.

"Mrs. Donald J. Rivard of Spring St. reported seeing the pair walking along Boston & Albany Railroad tracks that circle Benjamin Hill.

"She said the boy held the girl by the wrist and 'he was pulling her along.' She also said that he was carrying a rifle.

"At 1 a.m. today a local plumber reported seeing them in the Waterville section of the town, but a search of that area revealed no trace of them.

"And at 6 a.m. a resident told of hearing gunshots in a heavily wooded area near the junction of Rtes. 12 and 140.

"Acting Police Chief George S. Higgins said Caouette has had psychiatric treatment at Gardner State Hospital and at the Brattleboro, Vt., Retreat, a private mental institution.

"Higgins said the husky, 6-foot youth has a police record including a 1965 conviction for assault with a deadly weapon when he rammed his car into a Winchendon police cruiser. The boy was given a year's probation, said Higgins.

"Shortly before the girl was kidnapped, said Higgins, he was stopped while walking through the center of town with a rifle over his shoulder. Caouette was allowed to continue, said the chief, after he explained he had been out hunting.

"Last night the mothers of the missing pair were both taken to Winchendon Hospital and put under sedation.

"Police said both the girl's parents were at work when she was taken from their home. The father, Albert, is a machinist employed by Rodney Hunt Machine Co. in Orange. They also have two younger daughters."

The drama finally came to an end the

next day when Caouette, desperate with hunger, sent Marie into the Depot Store with the intention of purchasing some victuals. The Associated Press reported the situation on August 20:

## SUSPECTED KIDNAPPER
## IS CAPTURED

"WINCHENDON, Mass. — A former mental patient was captured Friday with the 13-year-old girl he abducted from her home Thursday at gunpoint, police said Friday.

"Steven H. Caouette, 18, and Marie Couture, both of Winchendon, were found near Fitzwilliam Depot, N.H. Police said Caouette surrendered without a fight.

"Chief Webb Sherman of the Fitzwilliam police said the pair was spotted by George Dunton Jr.

"'He saw the two of them in a field near the general store,' Sherman said. 'I called the state police and the sheriff's department,' he said. 'They were taken into custody without trouble. The rifle wasn't fired.'

"Caouette and the girl were taken to Keene, N.H., police headquarters."

One is tempted to think of the case of Charles Starkweather and Caril Ann Fugate, in which eleven people were killed in a similar situation. Here, however, we can be thankful that the crisis came to an end with nobody ending up getting murdered. As it turned out, Marie Couture was returned to her parents and home, and Steven H. Caouette returned into custody, no doubt being observed for further mental instability.

• • •

Another case of extreme jealousy resulted in far more serious consequences, as it prompted a man to try to kill his wife and then attempt suicide. The fact that the perpetrator and the victim both apparently survived their wounds must be attributed to bad aim, rather than any bouts of conscience.

The husband in question was one Charles E. Champney, a resident of State Line, just on the border of Fitzwilliam and Winchendon, Massachusetts. In the summer of 1887, Champney's wife had been working at the farm of Joseph Damon, and he was beginning to entertain thoughts that she was unfaithful.

This resentment simmered for some time; and, by the end of June, Champney decided he would confront his wife once and for all.

On one Saturday, at about 11:30 in the morning, he tramped down what is now Route 12, and encountered his wife, on the way to work. Well, a heated dispute soon followed, with the couple yelling at each other in the middle of the road.

At some point, Champney produced a .32 caliber pistol, and aimed it at his wife. Seeing he was in earnest, she attempted to flee the scene. It was, however, just a little too late. As she ran, Champney fired twice at his wife. One bullet hit her squarely in the back of the head and went down the neck, while the other lodged behind her skull. Even then, she continued running, hoping to escape her husband's wrath. He let off a third shot, which grazed her ear. She managed to make it to a nearby house, where she sought help.

As soon as his wife was out of sight, Champney began to realize the enormity of his own position. He ran into the woods next to the road, and thought things over for a bit.

After a while, he came to the conclusion that suicide was the only way out. He fired a shot into his own forehead, penetrating his skull. That, however, didn't kill him, and he decided to move on.

Eventually, he made his way to his brother's house, where he explained the whole situation. We don't really know if he received the degree of sympathy that he expected, but it is clear that he was still on a suicidal bender. He decided to shoot himself again, this time in the chest. The shot went through his left breast and passed through the lung, penetrating within an inch of his heart.

A surgeon was called in, who removed the bullet from Champney's back. He also extracted the earlier shot from his forehead.

When last heard of, Champney was lying in critical condition. His wife, however, had made a significant recovery, and was able to sit up, unassisted.

You can see Champney's grave in the Fitzwilliam Village Burial Ground. His wife is there, as well, buried under her maiden name, Bessie Tibbetts. Bessie passed away in 1898, at the age of 46. Oddly, although town records indicate her birthdate as being 1852, the stone states that she was born in 1882. Of course, this would have made her five years old at the time of the assault. One is tempted to wonder whether the injuries Mrs. Champney suffered at the hands of her husband hastened her demise.

Charles Champney, on the other hand, lived until 1926. It's entirely probable that he served some jail time for his homicidal shenanigans, but I don't have direct proof of that. The fact that he outlivd his wife by nearly 30 years, however, lends a certain amount of truth to the adage that only the good die young.

A visibly bruised and
battered Dorothy Kelly
attends a press conference
in April of 1977, having
survived a horrific airline
accident in Tenerife.

# EIGHT
# A VERY
# BRAVE WOMAN

Most of us generally don't think of ourselves as heroes. We go through our daily lives with little idea of how we would react if suddenly confronted by tragedy. There is, however, a facility within us all when, faced with a critical situation, we find ourselves acheiving feats of which we never expected we could be capable.

Such a situation faced 36-year-old Fitzwilliam resident Dorothy Kelly, a stewardess for Pan-American Airlines, on March 27 of 1977, when she was tending what was supposed to be a routine flight from Tenerife, in the Canary Islands.

The 747 at which she was stationed was parked on the runway at Los Rodeos Airport. Unbeknownst to her, events were quickly taking over which would lead to one of the most horrendous aviation disasters in history.

A bomb explosion at Gran Canaria Airport, with the threat of a second bomb, prompted many aircraft to be diverted to Los Rodeos Airport. Among these were KLM Flight 4805 and Pan Am Flight 1736. At this time, air traffic controllers were forced to park a great number of airplanes on the taxiway, effectively blocking it. Exacerbating the situation was the fact that, while authorities were waiting to reopen Grand Canaria, a thick fog settled over Tenerife, obliterating visibility.

When Gran Canaria eventually reopened, it was decided that both of these 747s should taxi on the runway in order to get into position for takeoff. The fog was so thick, however, that neither could see the other, and the controller in the tower was unable to see the runway.

The airport wasn't equipped with ground radar, and the only way that the controller could figure out where the planes were was by voice reports over the radio.

Things quickly went south, and the KLM flight attempted to take off while the Pan Am flight was still on the runway. The resulting collision destroyed both aircraft, killing all 248 aboard the KLM flight and 335 of the 396 aboard the Pan Am flight. Sixty-one people aboard the Pan Am flight survived, including the pilot and the flight engineer, due in no small part to Mrs. Kelly's heroic efforts. We have this account from the April 2 edition of *The Boston Herald:*

### PASSENGERS FOUGHT TO RETURN TO FIERY JET IN RESCUE EFFORT

"NEW YORK (AP) — A Pan American stewardess who survived the worst airline disaster in history says crew members had to fight with some passengers to keep them from going back into the exploding plane to help others.

"'There were horrible screams inside

The burnt-out hulk of
the Pan Am 747 sits on
the runway of the Los
Rodeos airport at Tenerife
after a horrific collision
with KLM Flight 4805 in
March of 1977.

the cabin,' said 36-year-old Dorothy Kelly.' There were people being severely burned and families trying to get back into the plane to help them. Metal was flying in the air around us as the plane exploded.'

"Mrs. Kelly, of Fitzwilliam, N.H., was one of six survivors, who returned here Thursday night following Sunday's disaster at Santa Cruz de Tenerife in the Canary Island when 577 died.

"The stewardesses were rushed past waiting reporters, but Mrs. Kelly returned and held a brief news conference on her recollections of the holocaust.

"Her arm in a cast, her face scratched and bruised and her eyes showing the strain of the tragedy, Mrs. Kelly said her first impression after the Pan Am plane and th KLM jet collided on the runway was 'a lot of wind, a lot of noise.'

"'Things were flying all over the place,' she said 'I could see the sky above.'

"As the plane burst into flames, she said, some passengers were blown out and others jumped.

"'On the right side directly behind

A shot of the devestation on
the runway of Los Rodeos
airport, Tenerife, in the wake
of the collision.

me,' she recalled, 'the girl that I had just looked at prior to the crash disappeared. I later learned that she got out without a scratch.'

"Mrs. Kelly said she felt the floor give way under her.

"'It was about a 25-foot jump into ragged metal below,' she said, 'and my shoes were gone...I managed to get down and out of the aircraft.'"

Further details of the accident and its aftermath were revealed in the April 1 edition of the (Washington D.C.) *Evening Star:*

"The gear was flown out on a Spanish military plane for a flight to Washington and a read-out Monday.

"Both Pan American and KLM prepared to fly the charred bodies of the victims home for identification and burial by the weekend. Most of the 69 persons who survived the collision have already been flown home to the United States.

"Yesterday, four surviving stewardesses arrived in New York with two passengers who lived through the collision. One of them, Dorothy Kelly, 36, of Fitzwilliam, N.H., said the crew members tried their best to evacuate as many passengers as possible from the burning plane and had to fight with some to prevent them from returning to the plane to help others.

"Twelve badly injured survivors at Brooke Army Medical Center, a renowned burn treatment facility in San Antonio, Tex., were in 'remarkably good spirits' and doctors said they had started what is expected to be a long recovery period.

"A medical official said the first two days were the most important in surviving extensive burns — but he also said infection could interfere with recovery at almost any point.

"The bodies at Tenerife, tagged but not identified, lay in rows of wooden coffins in a hangar. Both airlines said they would fly their own dead home.

"The tail of the KLM jet, the biggest piece of debris remaining from the Dutch plane, was pulled off the runway by cranes yesterday and workmen turned to the Pan Am wreckage.

"Announcing that cockpit voice recorders and digital flight recorders —black boxes — from both planes had been turned over to investigators by Spanish authorities, chief U.S. investigator William R. Haley called the electronic evidence 'important and valuable information.'

"He said the black boxes would tell American, Dutch and Spanish investigators the speed and direction of both planes and confirm interpretations that the KLM jet was airborne just before the crash."

Naturally, with a tragedy of this magnitude, lawsuits must inevitably follow; and the litigation was hot and heavy almost immediately. As it turned out, there were suits against both airlines totaling $2 billion.

A year after the accident, in April of 1978, Dorothy Kelly was recognized by the Department of Transportation, and given an award for heroism — the first time any such award was issued.

A long shot of the wreck
of two 747 planes at Los
Rodeos airport, Tenerife.

A report on the ceremony comes to us from the April 2 edition of the *Dallas Morning News:*

## AGENCY CITES STEWARDESS FOR HEROISM

"Washington (UPI) — Dorothy Kelly, a stewardess on the Pan American World Airways jet that crashed in the Canary Islands, has won the first award for heroism that the Department of Transportation has ever issued.

"A statement said Ms. Kelly, of Fitzwilliam, N.H., 'risked her life to save passengers and crew members in the fiery Canary Islands ground collision of two 747 jet planes.' The March 27, 1977, crash at Tenerife airport killed 577 people.

"The award, created in 1975 is the highest issued by the Transportation Department.

"Four other Pan Am crew members won the Federal Aviation Administration's award for distinguished service: first officer Robert L. Bragg, Howard Beach, N.Y., and three flight attendants,

Carla Johnson, Oyster Bay Cove, N.Y.,
Suzanne C. Donovan, Harrisburg, Pa.,
and Joan Jackson, Nashville Tenn.

"Transportation Secretary Brock
Adams said, 'Amid the fire, explosions
and flying debris following the crash,
and despite her own head injuries and
a broken arm, Kelly directed passengers
to safety and repeatedly returned to the
burning wreckage to assist injured passengers and crew members.'

"Adams quoted pilot V. F. Grubbs
as saying, 'Although I wanted to stop,
she continued to pull me ... there was
blood coming from a wound in her forehead and it was trickling down her face
... Without question, I owe my life to
Dorothy.'

"Bragg was honored for moving
critically injured passengers despite his
own broken ankle.

"Ms. Donovan and Ms. Jackson
were trapped temporarily in the fuse-
lage. They freed themselves and helped
passengers with them crawl to safety.

"Despite an increase in the fire's

intensity, Ms. Johnson helped sunned passengers escape the wrecked plane."

Of course, the news of this award sparked renewed interest in the tragedy, and the *Boston Herald* sent a reporter out to Fitzwilliam for an exclusive interview with Kelly. Having had a year to gather her thoughts, she gave an extensive account of her ordeal. Here is the piece, published in their April 2, 1978 edition:

### INTO THE FLAMING WRECK: A BRAVE STEWARDESS WINS A MEDAL

"By BARBARA RABINOVITZ

"Staff Writer

"A year ago last week, Dorothy Kelly was lying in a hospital in Tenerife in the Canary Islands. She had a fractured skull and a broken arm, injuries she suffered in the worst airplane crash in aviation history.

"A 36-year-old flight attendant for Pan American Airways, she had ignored her wounds to repeatedly rescue passengers from the burning Pan Am 747 jet after its collision with another 747 on a

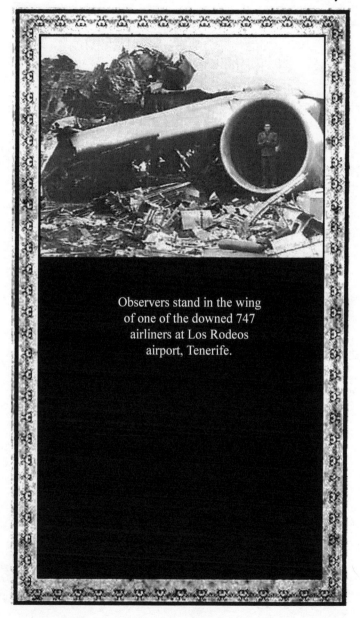

Observers stand in the wing
of one of the downed 747
airliners at Los Rodeos
airport, Tenerife.

fogbound Tenerife runway.

"Last Monday, on the first anniversary of the disaster, Kelly, one of 62 survivors of the crash that claimed 581 lives, was honored for her rescue efforts.

"She became the first recipient of the U.S. Transportation Dept's Heroism Award, the highest bravery award given out by the agency.

"At the presentation in Washington, Transportation Sec. Brock Adams praised Kelly for 'her heroic acts that endangered her own life.'

"Kelly, on return to her Fitzwilliam, N.H. home the other day, said somewhat self-effacingly that she 'appreciated the recognition.'

"Those she helped that late afternoon of March 27, 1977, more than appreciated her help.

"'Without question, I owed my life to Dorothy, who, at the risk of her own life, pulled me to safety despite her own injuries,' the pilot of the Pan Am plane, Victor F. Grubbs, said after the accident.

"Kelly had spotted Grubbs, badly

Dorothy Kelly, photographed
for the April 2, 1978 edition
of *The Boston Herald*.

burned, lying on the grass under the aircraft. 'I started pulling him away,' she said, 'but he said he couldn't go on. I kept tugging him, and just as we got a safe distance, the engine exploded.

"On a medical leave of absence since the accident, Kelly is still troubled with her injuries. 'I have pain in my head every day,' she said, 'and I have tendon and nerve damage from the break in my (left) arm.' (She's left-handed.)

"Her head injury occurred when she was hit by a piece of the plane's super-structure after the other 747 jet, a KLM Royal Dutch Airlines aircraft, sliced off the second-floor lounge area and roof of the cockpit and ripped open the rest of the Pan Am jet.

"Kelly had been standing in the front section on the main cabin floor.

"'My first thought was to reach up and get an oxygen box, because I knew there would probably be smoke imme-diately. My second thought was that the airplane was blowing up and an oxygen box would blow up with it. And my third though was there was no ceiling to reach to get a box.

"'At that point,' she said, 'I realized I had to get out.'

"As the air began to thicken with smoke, she noticed a hole about 10 feet above the floor of the other side of the cabin picked her way over tangled metal and debris and onto the top of the aircraft. She found herself about 25 feet above the ground.

"'It was higher than the second story of my house,' she said. 'I was afraid. There was all this jagged metal around.'

"She jumped and landed on a grassy spot. 'That's when I think I injured my arm,' she said. 'I landed on my feet but had supported myself with my arm.'

"Flames were leaping from the Pan Am plane. The KLM jet had 'exploded into many pieces,' Kelly remembered.

"'My head was cut and bleeding, and I couldn't see out of one eye where the blood was congealing.'

"Even with her vision limited, she could see passengers standing around the Pan Am plane. Others lay on the ground moaning in pain.

"'From the emergency training we received, we learned we have to get people away from the aircraft because of the danger of fire,' explained Kelly, who has been a flight attendant with Pan Am for 11 ½ years.

"'I felt impelled to get the people who were alive away from the plane. Some of them had broken bones or were in shock and couldn't move.

"Fearlessly, she darted back to the flaming jetliner and helped move passengers away from the craft. 'I had just enough time to get away (from the explosions) each time,' she said.

"Later, she was taken — in one of the last ambulances to leave the accident scene — to a hospital in Tenerife where she was treated for four days before being flown back to New York.

"In retrospect, she realizes she took many risks, 'but I thought I was using my best judgment. In a situation like that, you feel you can't leave those people. You know they don't know what to do and you do.'

"Some of the deaths possibly could have been prevented, according to Kelly. While many people died because they could not move themselves out of the plane, she said, 'we were told later that people had been milling around the aircraft talking about what happened as explosions engulfed the plane.'

"More attentiveness by passengers to safety measures demonstrated by flight attendants before takeoff might avert fatalities, in Kelly's opinion. 'People don't pay attention to those instructions we give,' she noted.

"Although her memories of the crash are vivid, Kelly is not letting the experience deter her from continuing with her career. She hopes her health will improve enough in about six months so that she can return to flying.

"Meanwhile, she is putting her artistic talents to use — she received a degree in art from the College of St. Elizabeth in New Jersey — by taking courses at

Franklin Pierce College in Rindge, N.H., for work as an interior decorator.

"She and her husband, Paul, also 36 and a Pan Am pilot, share in interest in photography.

"The 26 acres around their four-bedroom house, where they live with two cats, are the site of a pistol range, track range, tennis court and an air strip.

"They own a Cessna 185; Dorothy has a private pilot's license. But since the accident, she hasn't done much air traveling.

"Admitting to some apprehension, she said: 'It will never be the same when I get on a plane.'

Modest as Dorothy Kelly appears to be, it is undeniable that she went above and beyond her duties in a time of crisis, and was responsible for saving the lives of a number of staff and passengers during an unthinkable crisis.

*Photograph by the author*
Memorial to Major Daniel T.
Hayden, hidden in the woods at The
Pinnacle in Fitzwilliam.

# NINE
# A TRAGEDY
# AT THE PINNACLE

One of the highest points in Fitzwilliam is an area of land known locally as "The Pinnacle." It lies along the side of Upper Troy Road, and is basically a warren of old lumber trails and the occasional house.

Out in the middle of the woods, in a spot that hasn't seen a road or trail in many years, there stands a huge obelisk, about 10 feet tall, with a rusted chain fence surrounding it. At the time it was erected, the slope of this hill was probably open pasture land, and access to the monument was undoubtedly an easy task. Over the last 177 years, however, the forest has reclaimed this bit

*Photograph by the author*
Close shot of the face of
Major Daniel T. Hayden's
memorial. Time and weather
has rendered the inscription
almost indecipherable.

of real estate, and access to the stone is now blocked by a thick tangle of trees, bushes, and rotted logs.

The inscription on this edifice is worn by the weather, to the point of being almost indecipherable. For those who know, however, it commemorates an ancient tragedy.

The memorial was actually erected back in 1838 by members of the Fitzwilliam Fire Department and other individuals of note in town. It marks the spot where one Major Daniel T. Hayden, 30 years of age, met his untimely death. Hayden was a man of considerable connections, being the son of Mr. Joel Hayden and the son-in-law of Phineas Reed, a Revolutionary War hero who had been one of Fitzwilliam's early settlers. Actually, Joel Hayden's house still stands on Upper Troy Road, a handsome reminder of a more genteel age.

On the morning of August 18, 1838, Hayden and a close friend decided to go hunting up on The Pinnacle. It was something they did often, and had no

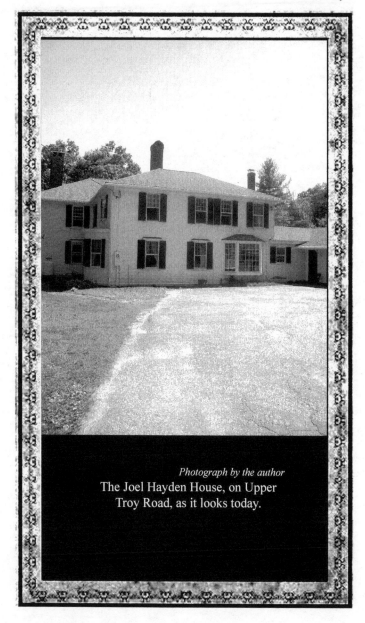

*Photograph by the author*
The Joel Hayden House, on Upper
Troy Road, as it looks today.

idea of the tragedy that would befall them before the day was out. The full details of what transpired that morning were reported in the September 7th edition of *The Farmer's Cabinet:*

"In Fitzwilliam, on the 18th inst., from the discharge of his own rifle, which he had been using, Mr. Daniel T. Hayden, aged 30 — son of Mr. Joel Hayden and son-in-law of Phineas Reed, Esq. The ball passed through his vest and cravat, which took fire — entered the left side of the chin, and passed out on the right side of his head. Death was nearly instant, and without struggle as could be. How the event was caused, may not certainly be known. — The rifle had a percussion lock. From examination it was found that some small stakes standing against a small tree, from some cause fell, and from the position in which he was standing, it is probable that one of these struck the hammer of the lock and threw it back far enough for its striking fire upon returning. — This appears nearly certain — much the most prob-

In Fitzwilliam, on the 18th inst. from the discharge of his own rifle, which he had been using, Mr. Daniel T. Hayden, aged 30—son of Mr Joel Hayden, and son-in-law of Phineas Reed, Esq. The ball passed through his vest and cravat, which took fire—entered the left side of the chin, and passed out on the right-side of the head and of the hat. Death was nearly instant, and without struggle as could be. How the event was caused, may not certainly be known.— The rifle had a percussion lock. From examination it was found that some small stakes standing against a small tree, from some cause fell, and from the position in which he was standing, it is probable that one of them struck the hammer of the lock and threw it back far enough for its striking fire on returning — This appears nearly certain—much the most probable of any way in which the sorrowful event can be accounted for. His neighbor and friend was within a few feet of him when done. Mr. Hayden was a very active and valuable young man. Though few may thus come to their end, yet this may be an instance strong to disclose that we are in 'death's oft', and that the day may have great events for us of which the morning knows not. •

Article from the September 7, 1838 edition of *The Farmer's Cabinet*, reporting on the accidental death of Major Daniel T. Hayden.

able way in which the sorrowful event can be accounted for. His neighbor and friend was within a few feet of him when done. Mr. Hayden was a very active and valuable young man. Though few may thus come to their end, yet this may be an instance strong to disclose that we are in 'death's oft' and that the day may have great events for us of which the morning knows not."

As Daniel was the breadwinner in the family, his death left his young wife, Sarah, in an untenable situation. She now had no visible means of support, and the creditors were moving in. How fast this occurred is illustrated in this notice from the December 5 edition of the *New Hampshire Sentinel:*

### NOTICE.

"The subscribers having been appointed Commissioners by the Judge of Probate for the County of Cheshire, to receive, examine, adjust and allow the claims of the creditors against the estate of DANIEL T. HAYDEN, late of Fitzwilliam, in said County, deceased, and

*Photograph by the author*
The grave of Daniel T. Hayden, located
in the Village Cemetery, Fitzwilliam.

six calendar months from the twentieth day of November, instant, having been allowed for the discharge of said duties, hereby give notice that we will attend for the purpose aforesaid, at Capt. James Godfrey's Tavern, in said Fitzwilliam, on the third Wednesdays of February and May next, from one to six o'clock, on each of said days.

"DEXTER WHITTEMORE,
MILTON CHAPLIN,
DANIEL SPAULDING,
Commissioners,
Fitzwilliam, Nov. 30, 1838."

Well, the writing was on the wall, as they say. By 1839, Sarah was unceremoniously booted off her property, as illustrated in this notice from the August 25, 1840 edition of the *New Hampshire Sentinel:*

NOTICE

"Is hereby given that the subscriber, on the 28th day of August, A.D. 1839, entered upon and took possession of the premises conveyed to him by Daniel T. Hayden, by this mortgage dated May 14, 1838, situated in Fitzwilliam village,

*Photograph by the author*
The grave of Sarah Reed, located in the
Village Cemetery, Fitzwilliam.

bounded on the land of Asa Brewer, Abel B. Robeson, Robinson Perkins and the subscriber, and also on the road leading from said village to Troy, containing about half an acre, for the purpose of foreclosing said mortgage.

"CURTIS COOLIDGE, Fitzwilliam, Aug. 15, 1840."

It gets really kind of fuzzy as to what happened to Sarah for the next 17 years or so. It's as if she just kind of drops off the historical record. Remarkably, the next time we hear of her is on New Year's Day, 1857, when it is recorded that she married noted local merchandiser Dexter Whittemore, and promptly decamped to New York City.

In the Amos Blake House, the home of the Fitzwilliam Historical Society, there is a photograph of a family reunion of the Whittemore Family, taken on Thanksgiving Day of 1872. By this point, Sarah had presented her husband with some 14 children, and had taken up the sobriquet of "Little Grandma" in the family. It's interesting to see her in this

*Photo courtesy the Fitzwilliam Historical Society*
Sarah Reed Hayden Whittemore,
photographed at a family reunion on
Thanksgiving of 1872.

new environment, comfortable in the bosom of her family.

One can only imagine the thoughts that were going through her mind; and whether or not her memories traveled back to the sad tragedy that took her young husband; and the lonely monument erected to his memory at the side of the Pinnacle.

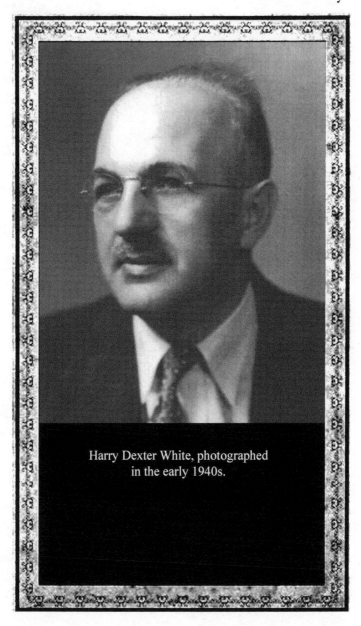

Harry Dexter White, photographed
in the early 1940s.

# TEN
# FITZWILLIAM'S RED SPY?

I have to admit to entertaining a considerable amount of trepidation when approaching the subject of Harry Dexter White. Nearly seven decades after his death at his cottage on East Lake Road, he remains a figure of contention. It is alleged by many that he was a communist spy, by others that he was just a naïve idealist. Whichever way I move on this one, I'm going to attract criticism from on quarter or another. Nevertheless, I shall persevere.

Harry Dexter White was born the seventh and youngest child of Joseph Weit and Sarah Magilewski in Boston on October 9, 1892. During the First World War, he joined the United States

Harold Ware, founder of
the Ware Group.

Army, where he was commissioned as a lieutenant and served in France in 1918. Upon his return home, he studied economics at Columbia and Stanford Universities. It was at Stanford that he received his B.A. in 1924 and his M.A. in 1925. He gained his Ph.D. in 1930 from Harvard University, and served as Professor of Economics at Laurence College in Appleton, Wisconsin. He was also an instructor in Economics at Harvard University.

In 1934, as he was being appointed to the Treasury Department, he apparently also began to become involved with a communist association known as the Ware Group. This organization was led by one Harold Ware, the son of a well-known radical, Eva Reeve Bloor. In November of that year, he became a principal economic analyst in the Treasury Department's Division of Research and Statistics.

It was during this period that White began advocating a program of international monetary stability, and was sent to

U.S. Treasury Secretary
Henry Morganthau.

England in 1935 to study international economic issues. At this point, he met with the noted economist John Maynard Keynes, who influenced him in stressing the issue of Anglo-American cooperation in economics.

In October of 1936, White became assistant director of the U.S. Treasury Department's Division of Research and Statistics, where he remained until 1938, whereupon he became director of the Division of Monetary Research. In 1941, he was appointed Assistant Secretary of the Treasury. Upon the entry of the United States into World War II, Treasury Secretary Henry Morgenthau put him in charge of all international matters for the Treasury Department.

In 1944, White drafted the U.S. blueprint for the International Monetary Fund, competing with Keynes' own plan, drawn up for the British Treasury. At the United Nations Monetary and Financial Conference, which took place from July 1 to July 22 at Bretton Woods, New Hampshire, White served as chief technical expert for the United States Government, delivering press summaries of the committee meetings.

In November of 1944, White became involved in the Morgenthau plan, a strategy by which the allies were to decide how to deal with Germany in light of an anticipated Nazi surrender. Basically, this plan called for Germany to partitioned into two independent states, its main centers of mining and industry to be internationalized or annexed by neighboring states, and all of its heavy industry destroyed.

The plan was discussed at the Second Quebec Conference on September 16th, where President Franklin D. Roosevelt and Henry Morgenthau persuaded British Prime Minister Winston Churchill to agree, which he did, with reservations.

Unfortunately, the plan was leaked to the press, with the result that German Propaganda Minister Josef Goebbels used it to increase resistance to the allies along the Western Front.

Things started to go south for White

in 1945. For one thing, Russia declined to participate in the International Monetary Fund. White, as an ardent supporter of the Soviet Union, was gutted by this development, and his dream of a global economy was shattered. At the same time, the FBI began sending reports to the White House naming White at the top of its list of individuals suspected of spying for the Russians.

In 1948, former communist spies Whitaker Chambers and Elizabeth Bentley accused White of providing them with classified information, which they would then pass on to the Soviets. On August 13, White testified before the House Un-American Activities committee to refute the charges.

At the end of his testimony, he returned to his summer home in Fitzwilliam, ostensibly to recover from his ordeal.

Harry Dexter White passed away at his cottage on August 16th, 1948, of what appeared to be a massive heart attack. The next day, the Associated Press published this obituary:

# Former Treasury Aide, Named In Spy Probe, Dies

FITZWILLIAM (N. H.), Aug. 17, (AP)—Harry Dexter White, one time treasury official whose name was brought into the congressional investigation of Communist spy rings, died here yesterday. He was 56.

White was stricken with a heart attack Saturday only a few hours after he returned to his Summer home from Washington, where he had testified before the house un-American activities committee.

Harry Dexter Ward's obituary, as published by the Associated Press on August 16, 1948.

## HARRY D. WHITE, ACCUSED AS RED, DIES SUDDENLY

"Fitzwilliam, N.H., Aug. 17 (AP) — Harry Dexter White, 50, former assistant secretary of the U.S. Treasury, who last week denied that he was a member of an 'elite' group in the Communist apparatus in Washington, died yesterday at his summer home.

"A heart attack, suffered Saturday, only a few hours after his return from Washington, caused his death, Dr. George E. Emerson said.

"White testified before the House un-American Activities committee that the accusations of Miss Elizabeth T. Bentley were 'unqualifiedly false.'

### ACCUSED

"Miss Bentley had testified July 31 that through White's high Treasury position, he had helped communist agents by pushing certain government employees toward key positions where they would have access to secret information.

"Before he became assistant secretary of the U.S. Treasury, White was department secretary of the U.S. Treasury. White was a department expert for a dozen years.

## SPECIAL STUDIES

"He went to Washington to make special studies for the Treasury department, and though little is known to the public, his duties were of financial importance to the world."

One would have thought this might have brought an end to the entire affair. Things, however, didn't turn out that way. At the time of White's death, two separate governments had been set up in Korea, one a communist dictatorship, supported by China and the Soviet Union to the north, and the other a democratic state, supported by western powers, to the south. It was an uneasy peace, and the conflict turned to full-fledged warfare when North Korea invaded South Korea on June 25, 1950. The United Nations condemned this act as an invasion, and became involved in the mess on June 27. The United States led a coalition of 21 countries in this intervention, providing about 88 percent of the military support. The bloodshed continued for the next three years, when the new President, Dwight D. Eisenhower, decided enough was enough, and pushed through an armistice. As far as the Americans were concerned, the war was over, and the troops were sent home.

Fear of communism back in on these shores had, meanwhile, hit an all-time high. In January of 1949, the Soviet Union successfully exploded an atomic bomb. An alleged spy ring involving the theft of atomic secrets had been uncovered by the FBI, and as a result, accused spies Ethel and Julius Rosenberg were executed in the electric chair on June 19, 1953 at Sing Sing Prison, Ossining, New York.

When Truman left office in January of 1953, opting not to run for a second term, the war still had six months to run its course. The moment he was out of the White House, a cadre of Republican senators, led by the infamous Joseph McCarthy, decided to go after him,

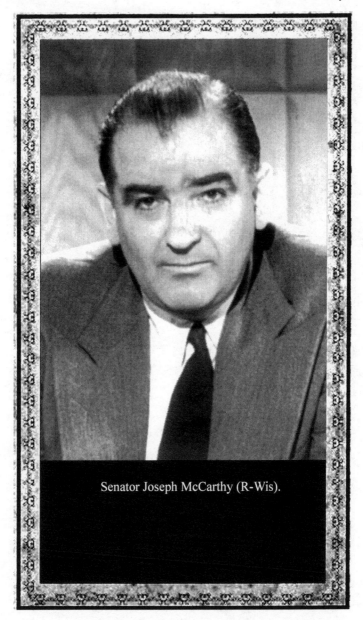

Senator Joseph McCarthy (R-Wis).

accusing the former President of having promoted White to the International Monetary Fund, in full knowledge of the accusations that he was a spy for the Soviets. An article in the November 15, 1953, edition of the *San Diego Union* gives us a taste of the paranoia that was so rampant at this time:

## TRUMAN PROMOTED SPY, SAYS MCCARTHY.

*Compiled from The San Diego Union's Wire Services*

"WASHINGTON, Nov. 11 — Sen. Joe McCarthy (R-Wis) said today former President Truman deliberately and knowingly appointed and promoted a Communist spy when he named Harry Dexter White to the International Monetary Fund.

"McCarthy, chairman of the senate permanent investigating subcommittee, told reporters President Eisenhower was 'being a gentleman' in commenting that he does not believe Truman knowingly harbored a Russian spy.

"'But if you look at the raw, harsh

facts, Truman did know White was a spy and promoted him,' McCarthy said. 'White was but one of many people in the Truman administration promoted and coddled.'

## PART OF PATTERN

"'It is part of a pattern that I have been trying to expose for three years. I feel that you can't be delicate when you are dealing with communists and the promotion of spies.'

"Sen. Ferguson (R-Mich) was opposed to calling Truman by subpoena, suggesting Truman might have been invited to give his version of the incidents after the facts had been gathered by congressional committee.

"Ferguson, however, criticized the Truman administration for its role in the White case and took issue with assertions of Democratic politicians that the exposure of White's Communist connections are dead coals.

## DEAD COALS, LIVE FIRE

"Dead coals usually are found on top a live fire,' Ferguson said. 'In this case, that live fire is communism.'

"Rep. Ciardy, (R-Mich), a member of the House Committee on Un-American Activities was claimed credit for suggesting the issuance of a subpoena to Truman, said the committee has made no charges and is calling on witnesses to find the facts.

"'The people have a right to know who plotted the White case and whether any remnants of the White crowd are still in government,' Ciardy said.

"Rep. Scherer (R-Ohio), also a member of the House committee, said he had not been consulted in advance but approved of the subpoena for Truman and would vote against its withdrawal.

### NOT TELLING TRUTH

"'It's obvious someday isn't telling the truth, isn't it?' Scherer asked.

"Rep. Walter (D-Penn), a member of the House committee, told reporters at a press conference Truman had no greater access to FBI reports on White in 1945 and 1946 than did Mr. Eisenhower, who was then Army chief of staff.

"Walter recalled that Atty. Gen. Brownell had said that FBI information on White was sent to Gen. Vandenburg on Feb. 26, 1946. Vandenburg then was head of Army intelligence. Reporters called Walter's attention to the fact that White had been confirmed for the monetary fund Feb. 6 that year and that Vandenburg did not receive the report until 20 days later.

### INFORMATION AVAILABLE

"Walter said that made no difference, because the same information about White was available to Mr. Eisenhower. Vandenburg is ill in Walter Reed Army hospital and could not be reached for comment.

"James E. Hagerty, White House press secretary, was asked whether Mr. Eisenhower had seen the FBI report on White. Hagerty conferred with the President and told reporters that Mr. Eisenhower had no recollection of having seen it."

At the same time that these allegations were being made public, it would appear that government agencies were going through White's belongings in search of evidence, even going so far as to breaking into his house in Fitzwilliam. For instance, we have this report from the November 16, 1953 edition of the *Seattle Daily Times:*

## SEARCH OF WHITE'S HOME HINTED

By The Associated Press

"BOSTON, Nov. 16 — The *Boston Globe* says in a copyrighted article that the summer home of the late Harry Dexter White at Fitzwilliam, N.H., was broken into last month. The newspaper suggests the burglar may have been looking for a typewriter or papers.

"Attorney-General Brownell has described White, a former assistant secretary at the Treasury, as a spy for Russia and has said President Truman knew it when he promoted him to be director of the International Monetary fund.

"The *Globe*, in an article by Charles L. Whipple, says the housebreak occurred sometime between October 26 and 29.

# Search of White's Home Hinted

By Associated Press

BOSTON, Nov. 16.—The Boston Globe says in a copyrighted article that the summer home of the late Harry Dexter White at Fitzwilliam, N. H., was broken into last month. The newspaper suggests the burglar may have been looking for a typewriter or papers.

Attorney-General Brownell has described White, a former assistant secretary of the Treasury, as a spy for Russia and has said President Truman knew it when he promoted him to be director of the International Monetary Fund.

The Globe, in an article by Charles L. Whipple, says the housebreak occurred sometime between October 26 and 29.

**Typewriter Issue Recalled**

"Ordinarily, it would seem from the White summer home?"

Whipple says Acting Sheriff Frank W. Walker doesn't think they were. "It doesn't look like the F. B. I.," he quotes Walker as saying. "I'd have known it if it were."

Whipple says Emil Puskala, who takes care of the house for White's widow, said he never saw a typewriter. Mrs. White, author of books for children, always "writes by hand," Puskala said.

The Globe also reports that the whereabouts of White's ashes —he died at Fitzwilliam of a heart ailment August 16, 1948— are unknown. After cremation, White's brother-in-law, Dr. Abraham Wolfson, a dentist who then lived in East Orange, N. J., took them in an urn, presumably to New Jersey, the newspaper says.

The burglary of White's Fitzwilliam Cottage, as reported in the November 16, 1953 edition of the *Seattle Daily Times*.

## TYPEWRITER ISSUE RECALLED

"'Ordinarily, it would seek to be just another break,' Whipple writes. 'but back in the long, sensational trial of Alger Hiss, there appeared among the so called 'pumpkin papers' one document that the government admitted was done on a different typewriter than the old Woodstock that convicted Hiss.'

"[Hiss, a former State Department official, was convicted of perjury in denying he had turned secret documents over to Whittaker Chambers, a communist courier. He was sentenced in March, 1952, to serve five years.]

"'Whittaker Chambers, the confessed ex-soviet spy, testified he might have obtained the documents from Harry Dexter White. A Federal Bureau of Investigation typewriter expert named Feehan told the court that it was typed on a 1936 Royal.

"'Was that what the 'burglars' were looking for? Or were they searching for more papers, hidden in the mattresses — one full-size and three small sizes —

taken from the White summer home?'

"Whipple says Emil Puskala, who takes care of the house for White's widow, said he never saw a typewriter. Mrs. White, author of books for children, always 'writes by hand,' Puskala said.

"The *Globe* also reports that the whereabouts of White's ashes — he died of a heart ailment — are unknown. After cremation, White's brother-in-law, Dr. Abraham Wolfson, a dentist who then lived in East Grange, N.J., took them in an urn, presumably to New Jersey, the newspaper says."

In all, the circumstances behind these events seem extremely suspicious, and, gathered together, almost smack of a conspiracy. For instance, what did exactly happen to Harry Dexter White when he came back to Fitzwilliam? His death seems just a little too convenient to be coincidental.

What is clear is that Joseph McCarthy and the House Un-American Committee had bigger fish to fry. Their objective was nothing less than to indict and try Harry S. Truman for treason. They might have succeeded, as well, if the tide of public sentiment didn't turn suddenly against them. Even President Eisenhower was wary of the mad-dog senator, declaring to his aides at one point that "I will not get into the gutter with this guy."

It seems there was no stopping McCarthy — but then hubris got the better of him, and he began to investigate the U.S. Army, searching for communist infiltrators. On March 9, 1954, pioneering television journalist Edward R. Murrow took it upon himself to attack the senator on his show, "See It Now." The scathing report was seen by millions of Americans, and spelled the beginning of the end for the HUAC.

On June 9th, McCarthy accused Fred Fisher, one of the junior attorneys at Hale and Dorr, a law firm owned by Joseph N. Welch, head council of the United States Army, of associating while in law school with the National Lawyers Guild, a group that FBI head J. Edgar

Joseph N. Welch, head council of the United States Army, whose confrontation with Senator Joseph McCarthy effectively ended the latter's career.

Hoover had sought to have designated as a communist organization. The altercation between the two men soon became heated, as Welch accused McCarthy of trying to destroy the young man's reputation.

"Until this moment, Senator, I think I have never really gauged your cruelty or your recklessness," Welch said. "Fred Fisher is a young man who went to the Harvard Law School and came into my firm and is starting what looks to be a brilliant career with us. Little did I dream you could be so reckless and so cruel as to do an injury to that lad. It is true he is still with Hale and Dorr. It is true that he will continue to be with Hale and Dorr. It is, I regret to say, equally true that I fear he shall always bear a scar needlessly inflicted by you. If it were in my power to forgive you for your reckless cruelty I would do so. I like to think I am a gentle man, but your forgiveness will have to come from someone other than me."

Undeterred, McCarthy continued to

grill Welch on the issue, drawing from him a response that would resonate with the American public and ultimately destroy McCarthy's career.

"Senator, may we not drop this?" Welch thundered. "We know he belonged to the Lawyers Guild. Let us not assassinate this lad further, Senator. You've done enough. Have you no sense of decency, sir? At long last, have you left no sense of decency?"

And that was pretty much that. When the Republicans lost control of the Senate in the midterm elections in November, McCarthy had to step down as chairman of the investigating committee. That December, the Senate convened censure hearings, and formally contemned him on a vote of 67 to 22 for conduct "contrary to Senate traditions."

McCarthy held onto his job, but died on May 2, 1957 of acute hepatitis at the Bethesda Navel Hospital outside Washington, essentially a broken man.

Harry Dexter White is largely forgotten by the general public these days, but remains a volatile figure among Cold War historians and economics majors. But, for a while there, he was a central figure in world politics, and drew the sleepy town of Fitzwilliam onto the world stage.

*Photograph by the author*
Emergency personnel prepare to remove a large
tree that fell onto Route 119 near Fitzwilliam
Depot during the summer of 2014. Torrential
rains over the previous week had loosened the
root system of the tree, rendering it unstable.

# ELEVEN
# WEIRD
# WEATHER

By the time that I moved to Fitzwilliam back in 2002, I had already resided in a number of cities, with radically differing climates. I've lived in the Midlands of England; Seattle, Washington; Boston, Massachusetts; and Fitchburg, in that same Commonwealth. In that city I acted as an editor of the *Sentinel and Enterprise*, a job that required me to stare at Main Street, for hours on end, while keeping an ear on the police scanner.

Now, if you ventured out onto the roof of the building, as I did, you could see some serious storms coming over Rollstone Hill with frightening inten-

## IN FITZWILLIAM.

The scene was still more melancholy. A girl, by the name of Betfey Clerk, about 16 years of age, was with her brother in a barn feeding calves with milk. She had fitten down on a fill of the barn, the lightning struck the barn, ran down a poft, and paffed to her head; the effects were terrible—the girl was inftantly killed, a blanket thrown over her had a hole.ftruck through it and took fire; her cloaths,and the barn were lighted in a flame. It is reported, although it is hardly credible, that the head of this unfortunate victim was confiderably torn by the lightning. This is certainly a very uncommon thing, and never to be expected, confidering that *animal matter* is fuch a powerful conductor of the electric fluid.

Account from the June 9th, 1801 edition of the *Farmer's Weekly Museum*, recounting the death of a 16-year-old girl, who was struck by lightning.

sity. As a matter of fact, I believe there was a case in the late 1980s, where lightning struck the steeple of the city church, bringing it down on the car of a nurse who was returning from her shift at the Burbank Hospital. She was, of course, killed on the spot.

As usual, I digress. The point is, I had never seen weather such as what we have here. I wandered around in the driveway for a while, just staring at the sky. It was a nasty gunmetal gray, and was boiling around like stew in a pot. I now understood why so many houses around here are outfitted with lightning rods.

Apparently, extreme weather is no stranger to these parts. Over the years, there have been many accounts of devastating storms, often destroying livestock, crops and even hapless bystanders. The earliest such account I could find comes courtesy of the June 9th, 1801 edition of the *Farmers' Weekly Museum*, published in Walpole:

### IN FITZWILLIAM.

"The scene was still more melancholy. A girl, by the name of Betley Clark, about 16 years of age, was with her brother in a barn feeding calves with milk. She had sitten down on a sill of the barn, the lightning struck the barn, ran down a post, and passed to her head; the effects were terrible — the girl was instantly killed, a blanket thrown over her had a hole struck through it and took fire; her cloaths, and the barn were lighted in a flame. It is reported, though it is hardly credible, that the head of this unfortunate victim was considerably torn by the lightning. This is certainly a very uncommon thing, and never to be expected, considering that animal matter is such a powerful conductor of electric fluid."

Good Lord. That's just horrifying. Imagine being 16 years old, going out to do your chores, just like any other day, when a bolt from the heavens comes down and basically incinerates you. It just goes to show that you never really know what could happen at any point.

Along with thunderstorms, Fitzwilliam has seen its share of hail. There was a particularly nasty example that visited the region in 1810, causing thousands of dollars of property damage and traumatizing the local population. We have an account from the May 21 edition of the *Vermont Republican*, which gives all the grisly details:

## GREAT HAIL STORM.

"On Friday, April 27, a cloud was formed near Northfield, which exhibited the most awful appearance, and discharged tremendous thunder and lightning, attended by a very high wind, and an uncommon storm of Hail,which occasioned a terrible devastation in the windows through the towns of Northfield, Warwick, Royalston, Fitzwilliam, and Rindge. Almost every square of glass which was on the windward side of the houses was broken. In the West Baptist Meeting House in Royalston, near three hundred squares were broken at the West End only. Hail stones were found an hour after the storm, which measured four inches and three quarters in circumference; and in general, they were the size of partridge's eggs. In many places over which the cloud passed, the hail fell to the depth of six inches, and it remained on the ground four or five days. The apple trees are very much damaged and stripped of the buds, so it is supposed they cannot produce any fruit next summer. The pines and other trees were also very much beaten and damaged. The greatest devastation was within about half a mile in breadth; and from what we have hitherto learned it appears to have extended about thirty miles."

The concept of snow storms, complete with thunder and lightning, is not one with which I am generally familiar. However, it does appear to have lain waste to Fitzwilliam in January of 1817. We have here an account from the January 20 edition of the *National Standard*, published in Middlebury, Vermont:

## SNOW STORM, ACCOMPANIED WITH LIGHTNING.

"The night of the 17th inst. was rendered remarkable by the very heavy thunder and lightning, uncommonly vivid. In this vicinity, these phenomena occurred about 12 o'clock at night. A moist snow accompanied with hail, fell at the time, and but little if any rain. We are informed that the new Meeting House in Fitzwilliam, (N.H.) was consumed by lightning in this storm, and that the dwelling house of Major Robertson, of the same town, was set on fire by lightning, but, happily extinguished."

Going through these old accounts, it would appear that a violent and dangerous storm hit Fitzwilliam every few years. In July of 1828, another vicious maelstrom descended on the village, endangering both man and beast. Here is how the *Boston Daily Advertiser* reported it in their July 21 edition:

"We continue to be visited with frequent and severe thunder storms. The storm which passed on Saturday morning was severely felt to the north, at New-Ipswich, Ashby, Fitzwilliam & c. We are informed that three horses in one stable were killed by lightning in

Fitzwilliam, and that a man in the act of cleaning one of the horses was struck down and somewhat injured at the same time. Two hogs were killed in Ashby. The storm of Saturday night, which was severe but of very short duration here, was felt with extreme severity in the towns abovementioned."

There is an old adage that lightning never strikes in the same place twice. Nonsense. After the meeting house burnt to the ground, a Unitarian Church was constructed on the same spot. Naturally there was trouble, as this account from the May 8, 1845 edition of the *Salem Register* will attest:

"We learn from the *Barre Patriot* that during a late thunder storm the Unitarian Church at Fitzwilliam was struck by lightning, damaging the building considerably. From appearances the bolt must have left the conductor, which was torn down, and descended one of the posts, which was much shattered, and the clapboards on that part of the house entirely stripped off. The meeting house formerly occupying the same ground was struck by lightning and burnt down, and this is the second time the present building has been endangered by the same cause."

Another severe hailstorm blasted the area during the summer of 1856. This time, in addition to breaking just about every window in town, the storm also destroyed the corn crop. We have an account from the August 28 edition of *The Farmer's Cabinet*, which vividly describes the damage:

## HAILSTORM IN FITZWILLIAM

"The severest storm of hail passed over Fitzwilliam village the 11th is the severest ever known by the oldest inhabitant. The storm began with a violent fall of rain and was soon succeeded by hail, the hailstones gradually increasing in size, were from one to two inches in thickness. Some of the large ones were picked up after the shower, one of which measured four and three quarter inches in circumference. Such hail continued falling until the ground

was entirely covered. Terrible havoc was
made upon the growing crops. Corn is
completely stripped or beaten down
and the English grain as effectively
threshed as by the blade of the husband-
man. Much damage is done to the fruit
trees, the limbs broken off and the bark
strangely battered. We already know
of some 4000 lights broken in this village alone. The storm passed eastwardly
toward Rindge where the violence of the
storm was even greater. The hail came so
thick as to cause the darkness of night
and the roaring of thunder. Hailstones
were there measured ten inches in
circumference!"

A severe storm hit the village again
in November of 1870, during which the
town house was struck by lightning and
severely damaged. Over in Marlbor-
ough, the same storm delivered a bolt
of lightning right into the public school
building, knocking the teacher insensible and seriously affecting the students.

During the hurricane of 1938,
Fitzwilliam was hit just as hard as the

other New England communities. At the time, there was a thriving logging trade in town, but the storm pretty much put an end to that. The woodlands were wrecked so badly that the owners couldn't find any landmarks, and logging came to an understandable end. Particularly hard hit was a grove of first growth pines owned by the Damon estate. These trees, reaching 125 feet in height, were completely decimated in the storm.

In 1953, a freak accident during a thunderstorm injured several firefighters, as recounted in this report from the June 23 edition of the *Springfield Union:*

### BOLT STUNS FIREMEN

"Fitzwilliam, N.H., June 22 — A bolt of lightning followed a stream of water being played on a burning house today, back to the hose, stunning fire fighters holding it. They were not seriously injured. Three houses were struck by lightning in this area during today's severe electrical storm."

For my own part, I recall the ice storm of 2008 with particular clarity.

*From the William and Elaine Pepe Postcard Collection*

An ice storm in Fitzwilliam, from an early 20th-century postcard.

That was when the power went out for several days, and we were forced to rely on hurricane lamps for light. Oddly, for these technically-obsessed times, we managed to somehow get by. We made tea on the propane stove, pulled out guitars and mandolins, and proceeded to play old folk songs throughout the those cold winter evenings.

In retrospect, it wasn't that bad.

Whaling ships in harbor at
New Bedford, from a 19th-
century photograph.

# TWELVE

# DEVOURED BY HIS SHIPMATES

Cannibalism. The mind recoils at the very mention of it. One of the last of the great taboos of mankind, one could hardly imagine that such a fate could befall any resident of this small town. Nevertheless, that is precisely what happened to G. Warren Dutton, the son of Calvin Dutton, a stonemason who oversaw work at Melvin Wilson and Son's granite quarry in Fitzwilliam.

At some point, Calvin Dutton decided to head out west with his son, and decamped to Minnesota. The son, however, decided to run away, and returned to this town, where his mother still lived. From here, he moved on to

New Bedford, Massachusetts, where he became a mate on a whaling ship. In 1861, however, he decided to desert the ship, and seek better employment. What he found, however, was a horrible destiny, doled out to him at the hands of his shipmates. There isn't anything I can really add to this narrative, so I will turn the entire account over to the January 9, 1862 edition of the *New Hampshire Sentinel:*

## HORRIBLE NARRATIVE.

*Sufferings and Cannibalism of an American Whaler's Boat's Crew.*

"The *St. John Daily News* of December 6th has an account of the sufferings of John F. Sullivan, of Hadley Falls, Mass., and his companions, deserters from the whaleships *Daniel Webster* and *Ansel Gibbs,* of New Bedford, in Cumberland Straits, on the 4th of August last. The narrative was written by Sullivan. The writer says that he had no reason for leaving the ship other that he was not sufficiently provided against the cold northern climate, and was afraid of dying by scurvy. The crew of the *Ansel Gibbs* complained of bad treatment. they were John Giles, boat-steerer, John Martin, Hiram J. Davis, Willard Hawkins, Thomas Colwell, Joseph fisher and Samuel Fisher, who, with Sullivan and his shipmate Warren Dutton, constituted the deserting party. They stole a boat from the *Ansel Gibbs* into which they managed to place a very small quantity of provisions, two guns and a little ammunition, and stood across the straits. They left the vessel in latitude 65 59, about five miles out from Penny's Harbor. On the fourth day out, they fell in with the barque *John Henry*, helmed by Capt. Cuddington, of New London, who offered to take them all on board, but they declined. He gave them some provisions, which were augmented by a duck and the hind quarters of a white bear, they managed to shoot before they made Resolution Island, where the provisions became nearly exhausted. On the 20th of August, at Cape Chadleigh, they had nothing but mushrooms and berries to live upon; and here Hawkins and Davis ran away from the party and carried away everything that was useful belonging to the boat. After an attempt to leave the place, which was prevented by stormy weather, they landed again and Dutton died of starvation. The narrative of Sullivan says —

"'The evening he died, Samuel Fisher proposed to eat him; he took his knife and cut a piece of the thigh, and held it over the fire until it was cooked. Then, next morning, each one followed his example; after that the meat was taken off the bones, and each man took a share. We stopped here three days. We then made a start; but the wind being ahead, we were compelled to put back. Here we stopped two more days. During that time the bones were broken up small and boiled in a pot or kettle that we had; also the skull was broken open, the brains taken out and cooked. We then got a fair wind, but as we got around a point we had the wind very fresh off shoe; we could hardly manage the boat; at last we drove on to an island some ways out to sea; we got the boat under the ice of it; but the same night we had a large hole stove into her. Being unable to haul her up, we stayed here eight days; it was on this island they tried to murder me.

"'The third day we stopped here, I was out as usual picking berries, or anything I could find to eat. Coming in I chanced to pick up a mushroom. I brought it with me, also an armful of wood to keep. While kneeling down to cook the mushroom, I received a heavy blow from a club from Joseph Fisher, and before I could get to my feet I got three more blows. I then managed to get on my feet, when Samuel Fisher got hold of my right arm. then Joseph Fisher got hold of my left arm; then Joseph Fisher struck me three more blows on the arm. I somehow got away from them, and, being half crazy, I did not know what to do. They made for me again. I kept begging them, for God's sake, to spare my life; but they would not listen to my cries. They said they wanted some meat and were bound to kill me. I had nothing I could defend myself with but a very small knife; this I held in my hand till they approached me. Samuel Fisher was the first to come towards me; he had a large dirk knife in his hand; his cousin was coming from another direction with a club and a stone. Samuel came on and grasped me by the shoulder and had his knife raised to stab me. I then raised my knife and stabbed him in the throat; he immediately fell, and I then made a step for Joe, but he dropped his club and went up to where the rest were. I then stooped down to see if Samuel was dead; he was still alive; I began to cry; after a little while the rest told me to come up — they would see that there was nothing more done to me. I had received four deep cuts in the head; one of the fellows dressed them for me, and washed the blood off my face. Next day Samuel Fisher died, his cousin was the first one to cut him up. His body was used up the same way as my unfortunate shipmate's.

"After a while we managed to repair the boat and left the island. We ran in where we thought was mainland, but it proved to be an island; here we left the boat, and proceeded on foot, walking about one mile a day. At last we reached the other side of the island in about four days; then we put back again into the boat. It took us four days to get back. When we got there we found the boat stove very bad since we left her. We tried to get round the island in her, but she sunk we got into her; we then left her and went back again to the other side of the island to remain there until we should die or be picked up. We ate our belts, boots, and sheaths, and a number of bear and seal-skin articles we had with us. To add to our misery, it commenced to rain, and kept up for three days; it then commenced to snow. In this miserable condition we were picked up by a boat's crew of *Esquineaux* on the 29th of September, and brought to Okoke on the 3rd of October. The missionaries did all that lay in their power to help us along, and provided us with food and clothing, and then sent us on to Nain where we met 'the doctor,' (Davis) who was picked up three days before we were. He reported that his companions died, and told many false stories after he was picked up.'

"The above thrilling narrative has the air of romance rather than reality, and some of the circumstances appear very improbable, but as the *Ansel Gibbs,* which arrived at New Bedford on the 11th of last November, reported the desertion of seven of her crew, with a whaleboat, in the Arctic regions, at the date above given, the main facts of the story are doubtless true. The misguided seamen suffered fearfully in consequence of their folly.

"The above account, from the *Boston Journal,* is confirmed in its essential features by Joseph Fisher, in a communication to the Journal of a later date, except that he denies attacking Sullivan with the intent to murder him, and that he was the first to cut up and eat the body of his cousin, and only did so at last from the certainty of otherwise dying.

"Dutton, whose horrible fate is above

described, it is believed was the son of Calvin Dutton, stone mason, resident of this town a few years ago. The young man's name was G. Warren Dutton, is known to have shipped at New Bedford. He was naturally a rather adventurous boy. A few years since, he clandestinely left his father in Minnesota, whither he had moved, and with little or no money found his way back to this town, to his mother, then residing in this town. His pleasing, sprightly address made him friends of steamboat captains and railroad conductors who forwarded him along without charge. So far as I know, he always bore a good character. His many schoolmates and acquaintances here cannot but shudder at his terrible fate.

"A.

"*Fitzwilliam, Jan. 3d, 1862.*"

And so ends this tragic and, dare I say it, distasteful tale. One thing is for certain — had young Dutton known of the horrible fate awaiting for him on the high seas, he might have well preferred to stay with his mother in Fitzwilliam.

*Photograph by the author*
The 1830s Connecticut shelf clock
that stands in John Fitzwilliam's
front room.

# THIRTEEN
# THE CLOCK THAT CAME HOME

Walking into John Fitzwilliam's house is something like stepping into another world. There are literally thousands of clocks throughout the space, in all shapes and sizes, filling every available shelf, table top, nook and cranny of the place. There's one thing for certain — he really loves clocks.

For nearly three decades, Fitzwilliam has been operating his little shop, "Clocks On The Common," where he meticulously fixes whatever problem any local resident might have with their timepiece. In addition to this, he has an almost encyclopedic knowledge of what makes these things tick, so to speak. Although he shares a surname with the town, that is

*Photograph by the author*
John Fitzwilliam, repairing clocks
in his workshop.

a matter of total coincidence. He actually grew up in Wellesley, Massachusetts, and only moved to these environs in 1987. It was while back in his hometown that he acquired a rather singular specimen, a Connecticut Shelf Clock, dating back to the 1830s. It was one of the first things he brought with him to town, and something that revealed some pretty odd coincidences, once he started looking into it.

"It was Halloween of 1987," he recalled. "I had just moved into the place, and was having some extensive renovation work done on the building. Since the front of the building was largely inaccessible, I knew that I wouldn't be answering the door. This gave me the chance to work on the clock, which I had bought with the intention of setting it up in this house."

The clockmaking industry in Connecticut began in 1773, when clockmaker Thomas Harland arrived in the colony to set up a shop in Norwich. Settling in, he made and repaired various timepieces consisting of intricate hand-

Eli Terry, who was instrumental in launching the Connecticut clock-making industry.

made brass gears. His apprentice, Daniel Burnap, learned a great deal on the job, establishing himself in South Windsor. In turn, a young apprentice by the name of Eli Terry signed on at the tender age of 14, and soon established himself as a phenomenon in the trade. By 1793, Terry had opened his own business, and four years later received the first clock patent granted by the US patent office. He went on to receive nine more patents over the course of his life.

"This was a really huge business back in those days," Fitzwilliam said. "The novel thing about this clock is that the movement parts were made of brass, whereas most clocks of that day were constructed of wood. So, it was a really expensive piece in those days. As a matter of fact, this particular clock was so notable that the famous clock historian Kenneth D. Roberts actually made a revision to one of his books in which it was featured."

As the evening grew on, and Fitzwilliam began to dissect his prize, he began

*Photograph by the author*
John Fitzwilliam's business,
Clocks on the Common, as seen
from the street.

to make a number of startling discoveries.

"The first thing I saw was was an inscription on the backplate, indicating that it had been thoroughly cleaned and repaired in Fitzwilliam by Warren Pratt in March of 1862," he explained. "Then I saw it had been repaired by William Flagg in 1857. That's when it really started to get interesting, as his property was right behind this house. If that weren't enough, my mother was related to the Flagg family, and several of their number are buried in the Village Cemetery. It was strange how these coincidences kept piling up."

Indeed, it didn't end there. Further examining the plate, he discovered that the clock had been repaired again in November of 1858, by P.S. Batcheller, who operated a store across the road, now occupied by Bloomin' Antiques.

"It was a very strange evening on the whole," Fitzwilliam said. "I realized that, from over a hundred years ago and 70 miles away, this clock had somehow managed to make its way home."

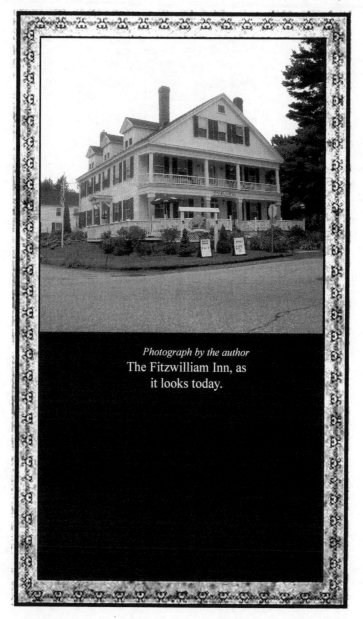

*Photograph by the author*
The Fitzwilliam Inn, as
it looks today.

# FOURTEEN

# SPIRITS AT THE INN

If there are any spirits to be found in this village, it would come as no surprise that they might be found at the Fitzwilliam Inn. No, I'm not talking about the liquid variety, although those are also readily available.

When David and Chelley Tighe purchased the property back in 2013, they quickly discovered that they had received far more than they had bargained for. In short, they had also inherited a number of very active ghosts.

It really shouldn't come as any surprise that the inn is haunted. After all, many of the town's residents have bellied up to the bar here for many generations.

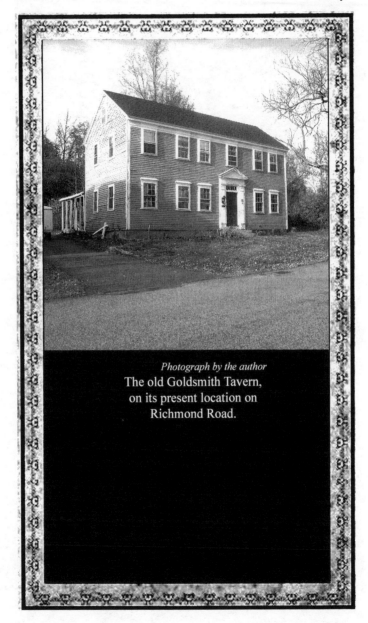

*Photograph by the author*
The old Goldsmith Tavern,
on its present location on
Richmond Road.

As we will discover, it turns out that many of them never really left.

The site of the inn has been occupied since 1794, when Tom Goldsmith built a small store here. Well, business was brisk, and he soon found himself with enough liquid funds to enlarge the property into a tavern, bearing the proud title "Goldsmith's." After a few years, David Perry took over the property, running it for a couple of decades under its new moniker, The Old Cheshire Hotel.

In 1843, it was decided that the building was no longer suitable for the kind of business that was being commanded, and the old Goldsmith tavern was moved down the road a few doors down Richmond Road. In its place, they built the imposing three-story edifice that overlooks the common to this day.

Despite all of the effort and expense that Perry put into the place, he decided that he wasn't going to hang around much longer. Accordingly, he placed the following advertisement in the December 11, 1844 edition of the *New Hamp-*

*shire Sentinel:*
## TAVERN STAND TO LET.

"The Old Cheshire Hotel, in Fitz-william, N.H., rebuilt, and will be let for a term of years, with or without the Farm connected with it. There are two large Barns on the premises, nearly full of Hay, which can be had with the premises at a fair price. Said hotel has just been completed, and is a thorough-built and commodious house, and the Stables are in complete repair. The Farm consists of about 80 acres, mostly Mowing and Tillage, and under a high state of cultivation.

"Immediate possession given. For further particulars, inquire of the subscriber, of or DAVID PERRY, DAVID FULLAM.

"Fitzwilliam, N.H. Nov. 26, 1844."

Whatever Perry expected to achieve with this advertisement evidently did not reach fruition, as he was in charge of the inn for the next 20 years, before handing it over to Oliver K. Wheelock. Under Wheelock's management, the inn continued to thrive and prosper. It was also, however, on his watch that one of the few recorded deaths at the inn was recorded. The whole sad tale was recounted in the August 21, 1889 edition of the *New Hampshire Sentinel:*

"Mrs. Bigelow, wife of Hon. Jonathan Bigelow of Cambridge, Mass., died at the Fitzwilliam-Cheshire Hotel Aug. 18. One week ago she was feeling ill and thinking she might feel better in country air she and her husband came to Fitzwilliam. She was quite exhausted when she reached here, and laid down on a bed which she did not leave alive. She had the almost constant attendance of Dr. Hubbard and Dr. Gleason came from Winchendon twice every day. Her anxious husband was unremitting in his attendance, but she survived only one week after her arrival at the hotel. Her disease was malignant dysentery. Mr. and Mrs. Bigelow are highly esteemed by all their numerous friends and acquaintances. This is the first death of a guest that has occurred at the Cheshire

If the B mt put:
If the B. putting:
Don't put : over a - der
You'd be an * it

*Photograph by the author*
Fitzwilliam Inn owner Chelley
Tighe, standing by the famous
rebus that has perplexed guests for
many years.

Hotel during the nineteen years that Mr. Wheelock has been its owner."

The inn changed hands again in 1900, this time becoming the property of Judge John S. Blair, who would operate the business for the next 46 years. Notably, it was he who had a particular rebus painted above the fireplace in the front room, which has perplexed and amused visitors for decades:

"If the Bmt put:
"If the B. putting:
"Don't put : over a -der
"You'd be an * 'it."

Before proceeding further, I would urge the reader to attempt to read these lines phonetically. Here's a hint: for capital B, read "grate B."

Give up? All right, then; here's the translation:

"If the grate be empty, put coal on
"If the grate be full, stop putting coal on.
"Don't put coal on over a high fender
"You'd be an ass to risk it."

Apart from managing the inn, Judge Blair was also extremely active in community affairs, especially when it came to farming. After all, the inn was, at this point, a fully functioning farm itself, with barns and fields providing meat, produce and dairy products for the guests. When the local turkey farms were diminishing, and residents were obliged to import birds from as far away as Texas, he hosted a meeting at the inn, in order to address this pressing issue. We have here an account from the January 9, 1922 edition of the *Boston Herald*, which recounts the particulars of that event:

"The 'turkey talks' began at 'The Tavern' in the afternoon, with John F. Blair as presiding spirit. It was agreed among all the participants that nothing too good could be done for the agriculture in this section of the country, and that 'back to turkey-raising' was a slogan especially needed at this ime.

"Quoting from The *Herald* article, the 'embattled farmers' asked why it should be necessary to rely on Texas, Wisconsin or even Vermont for such 'gobblers' as make their appearances in the markets hereabouts at Thanksgiving and Christmas times. Why not in this field break, the trusts, annihilate the middle men, escape freight rates, blast the cold storage and evade the government tax, all contributors to turkey scarcity and to the high cost of this historic bird all through New England?

"Fitzwilliam residents also 'looked backward' with many a sigh to the days in their own community when the turkey held the field against all other kinds of poultry. One old resident remembered the time when turkeys were so numerous that the breeders drove them to market along the roads.'I can remember great processions of them,' he said. 'An old gobbler would be put on ahead as leader, and the birds would march on to their destination for several days. At night time they would be turned into some field for shelter; at sun-up the start would be made again, and the procession would continue in that way until the destination was reached. Why can't we see that again?'"

Blair decided to get out of the inn-keeping business shortly after the Second World War, and the property fell into the hands of Frances and Kate Whitcomb. Loretta Lawrence ran it from 1957 to 1959, whereupon it was bought by Mary and Enoch "Red" Fuller. Mary wrote an amusing volume on her personal experiences at the inn in the book "A Horse in the Ladies' Room."

The inn has changed hands quite a few times since then, eventually becoming the property of Dave and Chelley Tighe. Almost upon taking possession of the building, the couple became acutely aware that there were some things that just weren't right with the place.

"One of the first things we noticed were pennies placed on top of the door jambs," Chelley Tighe said. "There is really no rhyme or reason why these appear, but they do."

Tighe said that the bar is a particularly active area on the ground floor of the inn, and has encountered a remarkably persistent spirit who continues to make his presence known.

"We believe this is actually the spirit of Pete the bartender, who passed away a few years back," she said. "When he was alive, he kind of ruled the roost around here. Shortly after we bought the place, I was standing at the bar, watching the hockey game with Tom, my bartender. Suddenly, I felt a very distinct tapping, three times, on my shoulder. I turned to Tom and asked what he wanted. He responded with 'what do you mean?' I responded that he had tapped me on the shoulder, which he denied. Well, there were some people sitting at the other end of the bar, and they told me that nobody had tapped me on the shoulder."

Tighe didn't think about this too much, until a couple of years later, when a new bartender was employed at the inn.

"This was a young man who had actually known Pete and worked with him," she said. "He told me that, whenever Pete wanted something from him, he would tap him on the shoulder three times, to get his attention."

Pete, the bartender who "ruled the roost" at the Fitzwilliam Inn for many years, and still haunts the bar years after his death.

That wasn't the end of the shenanigans at the bar, however. One day, according to Tighe, another employee was stacking bottles at the back of the bar, when they suddenly picked themselves up, flew over the woman's back, and landed on the floor.

"It was as if someone had literally thrown them across the room," she said. "We also have problems where the tops of the liquor bottles will pop off, all by themselves."

For a long time, the third floor was a hive of activity, as noises manifested themselves in the middle of the night.

"We were actually renovating that area at the time," Tighe said. "We had workmen here during the day, reconstructing walls and woodwork. Well, the guests would come down in the morning, complaining that they were working far too late — sometimes until two or three in the morning. I explained that we didn't have anyone working up there, but they insisted that they could hear people hammering and sawing away. Once the

*Photograph by the author*
The bar at the Fitzwilliam Inn,
one of the most active centers of
paranormal activity.

renovations were completed, however, everything just calmed down. It was as if whatever spirits were up there decided that we were doing well by the place, and just let us get on with it."

Another paranormal hotspot in the inn is the old apartment on the second floor, in the back, which now houses the laundry room.

"I was going up there one day, and could feel the hair literally rising on the back of my neck," Tighe said. "It was a very strange experience. Well, we had a visit from the Conscious Spirit Paranormal Group, headed by Theresa Harlow Sillanpaa, and they told us there was a spirit up there which was having a hard time crossing over. They told us it was the ghost of a woman who had committed suicide in that spot sometime in the 19th century. She had been very sad since her son died, and just wanted to be with him. They helped her cross over, and we haven't had any incidents in that spot since."

Theresa Harlow Sillanpaa confirms

A newspaper ad for
the Fitzwilliam Inn,
from 1955.

that the house is a very active area for paranormal activity, and has personally encountered a number of spirits within its walls.

"We were in the front parlor, where we encountered a spirit by the name of Mike," she said. "He came through very strongly on the Electronic Voice Phenomena equipment."

The history of the spirits predates the ownership of the Tighe family, however.

"There was a very strange event that occurred when the McManns owned the place," she said. "They had their kids over at the time, and they were sleeping on the second floor. In the morning, they confronted their parents and demanded to know why it was they were moving furniture around on the third floor. Well, the couple denied doing any such thing, and insisted that there wasn't even any furniture on that floor, to begin with."

Harlow Sillanpaa said that her investigation turned up a lot of activity throughout the building, and it remains

Theresa Harlow Sillanpaa,
founder and director of the
Conscious Spirit Paranormal
Group.

a hive of paranormal activity to this day.

At the time of this writing, around Halloween of 2015, Chelley Tighe has reported that the spirits on the third floor have renewed their spectral she-nanigans, with numerous guests complaining of being kept up at night by sounds of furniture being moved about on the floor above them.

So, if you happen to spend the night at the Fitzwilliam Inn, you can enjoy the fine food and drink, and the hospitality of the hosts. Be aware though — once you climb into bed and pull up the covers, you might get more than you reckoned for.